William James Dawson

Quest and Vision

Essays in Life and Literature

William James Dawson

Quest and Vision
Essays in Life and Literature

ISBN/EAN: 9783337205492

Printed in Europe, USA, Canada, Australia, Japan

Cover: Foto ©Thomas Meinert / pixelio.de

More available books at **www.hansebooks.com**

QUEST AND VISION

ESSAYS IN LIFE AND LITERATURE

BY

W. J. DAWSON

AUTHOR OF

The Church of To-morrow

This music crept by me upon the waters,
Allaying both their fury and my passion
With its sweet air; thence I have followed it,
Or it hath drawn me rather :—but 'tis gone.
No, it begins again !—*Tempest, Act I, Scene 2*

NEW YORK: HUNT & EATON
CINCINNATI: CRANSTON & CURTS
1892

CONTENTS.

ART AND TRUTH.

THE weary years, the summer's gold,
  Man's feverish joy and pain,
Pass like a dream, and all grows old:
  Tell me, what things remain?

Two names alone, and Truth is one :
  A face inscrutable,
With lips that neither laugh nor moan,
  Yet all things have to tell.

And Art the other : at the gate
  Of her old Paradise,
Whoe'er shall come, or soon or late,
  She opens to the wise.

We fade and pass : we fret our days
  In barren love and strife ;
But happier he who only prays
  Beneath the Tree of Life.

SHELLEY.

M R. RUSSELL LOWELL has used an admirable phrase about Wordsworth which is worthy of reproduction ; he has spoken of his " almost irritating respectability." Why respectability on the part of a poet should be irritating it is difficult to say, unless it be that the conventional tradition of poets is precisely the reverse of respectable. Poets, from Homer downward, have been more or less at variance with average society. They have not belonged to the sober, tax-paying, owe-no-man-any-thing type of humanity. Respectable citizens have habitually held them in suspicion, as persons of uncertain character, and presenting to the common eye no visible means of support. The Act of Parliament which reckoned the actor a vagabond marked the apotheosis of respectability, its concrete utterance, its definite and unalterable verdict upon all classes of men who live by the exercise or cultivation of the imaginative powers. One of the facts which philosophic moralists have to deal with is that, more often than not, men of imaginative genius have been open transgressors of the received laws and traditions of society. One has but to mention Burns, Byron, and Shelley —the three most commanding influences in the poetry of the century—in order to realize how grave a problem this presents. In each case we have the spectacle of immense genius allied to imperfect morals, and in the latter instances, not merely the outrage, but the defiance of morals. It is surely, therefore, a charming stroke of humor or satire that when at last there is vouchsafed to us a poet of unquestioned respectability, who actually knew how to collect taxes as well as pay them, who was in private life the most sober and decent of citizens, we straightway rebuke him for not being a chartered libertine, like the rest of his craft. Society, having constructed an ideal of what a poet is—namely, all that he should not be—expects every poet to conform to that most improper tradition. A poet without improprieties has no piquancy, and his very respectability becomes irritating. Thus is the poet impaled upon the horns of a most unjust dilemma: if vicious, he is a scandal; if virtuous, a bore.

We all remember the story of Theodore Hook being asked at a dinner-party, by an eager admirer of ten, when he was going to be funny. The question must have probed deep into the sore heart of Hook. There he sat, weighed down with bitter thoughts and shameful memories, in his brain madness, in his heart blackness and decay, only too conscious of the old age that made itself felt beneath the "paddings and washings," of the eclipse that was fast stealing upon his wit, of the hollowness of that bubble reputation he had made ; and then came this tiny questioner, with no cruelty in his childish heart, asking him when he was going to begin to be funny ! Was not that dinner the price paid for his jests? Had he not for years let himself out at that price to whosoever would ? The jester must needs jest, though his heart be breaking ; the actor who has just looked into the open coffin must nevertheless rush hither and thither in the farce, and say comic things in his funniest manner; it is no concern of society's that Hook is broken-hearted. There is no tyranny so cruel, and often so absurd, as the tyranny of tradition. This little story about Hook has many wide and obvious applications. The man who is celebrated as a wit must be funny on pain of extinction; a flash of silence is not permitted him; he is dragged at the heels of his own reputation, and cannot escape.

The class of men society has been pleased to identify as poets must, in similar fashion, abide by the traditional ideal society has set up. The actor may purge himself and his calling, and live in perfect nobility of life; but the mass of men will still persist in regarding him as an immoral person, whom the law recognizes as a vagrant; and to the vulgar mind the poet will still remain a person of unsound and unsafe life. You cannot persuade society that you are not what the tradition of your calling says you are; and the attempt only results in irritation and defiance.

As there is nothing more tyrannous, so there is nothing more unjust and even capricious, than the action of society toward its men of genius. It sets up one man and puts down another without adequate reason, or any reason at all. What it cheerfully condones in one it shrieks itself hoarse over in another. The temper of society toward social

offenses is an unknown quantity; no one can
with safety calculate the chances. It is just as
likely that the daring social iconoclast will become famous as infamous by his iconoclasm ;
between celebrity and ostracism there is but a
step. Society has no settled decalogue, no
Code Napoleon, no fixed standard of conduct
by which the iconoclast may measure his position or estimate his peril. It is more often than
not governed by the fitfulness of chance opinion,
and is drifted along the tide of mere circumstance. No better instance of this peculiarity
can be found than in the relative treatment of
Byron and Shelley. Both poets outraged the
traditions of society in the same direction, but
with difference of degree. The balance of degree
would be in favor of Byron and against Shelley. Byron never professed himself an atheist,
but Shelley did, and wrote a blasphemous
poem in favor of atheism. Byron never pro-
mulgated perilous doctrines of free love, but
Shelley dedicated his life to their promulga-
tion and shaped his conduct upon them.
Much as may be laid at Byron's door, nothing
baser can be alleged of him than the story
too well proved of Shelley's treatment of Har-

riet Westbrook. Byron's profligacy was the coarse and commonplace sort of profligacy that thousands of men of fashion in his own time and our time are guilty of. It would have passed unnoticed in a period so corrupt as the period of the regency but that he himself chose to publish it, to magnify it, and to gloat over it. Shelley was a sensualist, but not a profligate. He was as eager to blazon his sensualism as Byron his profligacy. In one of his longest and finest poems he approves of and glorifies incest. The difference between Byron's and Shelley's treatment of passion is that one treats it with coarse realism, while the other invests it with a subtle glamour. Byron knows he is wicked, and his transgression is ever before him; Shelley acknowledges no sin, and stands naked but not ashamed in his misdoing. The verdict of society upon the pair is one of the most anomalous in the history of literature. Byron is dismissed as a monster; Shelley has been recognized by one of his latest students as one who, under favoring circumstances, might have been the saviour of the world.

Not long since a poor woman, an habitual

drunkard, informed a magistrate that she believed she had no soul. She was an exception to the entire human race; she was destitute of what every other human being possessed. It was a flash of grim bitterness; the humiliation of despair could sink no lower. Let us for a moment try to conceive the possibility of such error on the part of the Creator; what sort of tragic abortion would this solitary soulless creature be? Certainly no despairing creature. Not having a soul, she would not feel the need of one, or be able to realize its existence. She would be destitute of conscience and moral sense. Things morally abhorrent would present no repulsiveness to such a being; the foul would simply be a different sort of fair; good and evil, hallowed and unhallowed, pure and infamous things would present merely so many interesting phenomena, and would be regarded with the same impassive curiosity. The proportion of moral things would be lost, or rather would never have existed. It would be vain to expect moral conduct from such a being; impulse and desire would be the only guides of conduct. The just laws which regulated ordinary mortals

would naturally appear a useless and cum-
brous tyranny. To admit such a being into
the society of ordinary creatures would constitute a constant peril. What safeguard would
there be for the preservation of honor, truth,
or chastity in the presence of one who was de-
void of that primal sense which comprehends
what these abstractions mean? Thus one
might push the speculation in many direc-
tions, and arrive at various grotesque and
tragic deductions. A powerful imagination
might so treat this conception in the realms of
fiction as perhaps to make it one of the most
fascinating of literary studies.

It is far from me to describe Shelley as a
man without a soul, but if one can conceive a
great poet almost destitute of all but rudi-
mentary moral sense Shelley might very well
embody the conception. Let any one take the
extraordinary story of his conduct to Harriet
Westbrook, Mary Godwin, and Jane Clairmont,
or rather the portion of the story which be-
longs to the relation of the three women to
each other. He leaves Harriet for no tangible
reason except that he has discovered she is
only a " noble animal," who does not properly

share his poetic sentiments. He then induces, with great difficulty, Mary Godwin, a girl just over sixteen, to leave her father's house with him. When they fly he is not content to rob Godwin of Mary, but actually takes Claire with them also, apparently for no other reason than that she would be an interesting companion. Then, to complete matters, when he has lived a few weeks with Mary, and under the same roof with Claire, he writes the forsaken Harriet a long and loving letter, suggesting that she shall join them, that they may all be happy together. On his return to London he visits Harriet as if nothing had happened, and thinks it would at least be a very admirable arrangement for Harriet and Mary to know each other. He aids and abets Claire in becoming the mistress of Lord Byron. Finally, within less than three weeks after the body of Harriet Westbrook has been found in the Serpentine, Shelley has married Mary Godwin.

If such a net-work of episode as this were introduced in fiction every critic in the kingdom would declaim against the monstrous improbability of the plot. One can very well fancy the sort of review that would be written.

2

" Before the author of this volume takes another flight in fiction," we can hear the wise
reviewer saying, " it will perhaps be well for
him to consider the following observations :
Seduction is unfortunately not uncommon, but
young men of two-and-twenty do not frequently forsake their wives after two years of
marriage, under plea of incompatibility of literary taste, and straightway seduce girls of
sixteen while sharing their fathers' hospitality.
When a man is base enough to seduce a young
girl he does not usually invite her sister to
accompany her in her flight from her father's
house, that she may become a daily witness of
her shame.   Neither is it common for such a
man to wish his deserted wife to live with his
mistress and to connive in bringing to shame
the sister of the mistress he has abducted.
And it may, perhaps, have come within the
knowledge of the author of this book, in his
observation of society, that even the most
hardened of profligates would be slow to outrage public decency to the extent of marrying
his mistress in less than three weeks from the
day on which his wife has committed suicide.
There is a secrecy in vice, a certain honor in

passion, a decency in sensuality, which forbid
such acts as these. Only a delirious fancy
could invent them and a morbid mind conceive
them. We beg to assure the author that in
real life such things do not occur," etc. To
do justice to the novelists, it may be said that
no novelist has yet invented such a plot as
this. But this is the clear, truthful, and un-
biased statement of what Shelley actually did.
He does not appear to have realized that there
was any incongruity, any unreasonableness, or
still less any shamefulness, in his conduct.
There was no malicious wit in his letter to
Harriet ; he sincerely imagined he had invented
an admirable arrangement for the comfort of
all parties when he invited her to live with
Mary and Claire. On his part it was simple
obtuseness, the entire lack of common perception. There is no sign that he recognized
either the absurdity or wickedness of his pro-
posals, that he even experienced any contrition
or remorse for the wreck of Claire's life or the
death of Harriet. Byron had too keen a sense
of the ridiculous ever to have been involved in
such an imbroglio as this, and too great a faculty for remorse not to have suffered bitterly

in its contemplation.   But to all this Shelley
was indifferent ; he looked upon it, but there
was no speculation in those orbs.   He went
placidly on his way wrecking and destroying
the lives of others as a child might amuse himself in a garden by trampling down the rarest
flowers, in pure gayety, and with no knowledge
of the damage he was doing.   Is not the most
charitable assumption in such a case that the
wrecker is morally insane, that he is deficient
in, or destitute of, all that constitutes the
moral sense ?

The most remarkable circumstance about the
moral errors of Shelley is not so much his own
indifference to them as the indifference of his
contemporaries and critics.   In one sense his
contemporaries were not indifferent ; undoubtedly Shelley did enough to make many people
dread his influence and hate his name.   He
tells us that in Rome he was regarded by all
who knew or heard of him as a rare prodigy of
crime and pollution, whose very look might in-
fect.   But, nevertheless, there was a curious
purity about Shelley, the existence and depth
of which was recognized by those who knew
him best.   Byron said he was the purest man

he ever met. Byron may not be the best witness on such a subject, but Leigh Hunt, at all
events, is a most respectable witness—a man
of conventional ideas on all subjects except
the financial obligations of literary men—and
there is plenty of evidence that Shelley impressed him in precisely the same way. Hazlitt did not like Shelley, but the worst thing
he can say about him is that he has a maggot
in his brain, a hectic flush, a shrill voice, and
the general aspect of a religious fanatic. With
all the new weight of evidence which Mr.
Jeaffreson has accumulated and the malicious
ingenuity with which he has applied it, it is
impossible to believe that Shelley was actuated
in his relations with women by the brutal selfishness and coarse passion of the ordinary be-
guiler of the sex. He was as completely sincere in his advocacy of the free contract and
his hatred of marriage as the Mormon fanatic
is in favor of polygamy. It is surely not un-
reasonable to suppose that a Mormon may be
a man of pure mind, of upright conduct, even
of pious spirit, in spite of his eccentricity of
having more wives than other people. Indeed,
it is a common statement that in Salt Lake

City ordinary profligacy is unknown. Precisely
in the same way Shelley, while holding odious
opinions which in the estimation of most civil-
ized people would sap, if carried out, the very
foundations of society, was himself a man who
impressed others by the almost virginal purity
of his character. People who were horrified by
his writings could scarcely believe they saw the
man whose name was a portent, in the fair and
gentle youth, of almost girlish aspect, whose
ordinary speech was set to a higher music than
other men's, and whose ordinary life was unsullied by a single blot of common profligacy.
As we have already said, he was not a profligate, and it is almost too much to call him a
sensualist. It would be truer to describe him
as morally insane upon certain subjects, the
chief of which was the marriage relation. This
was the maggot in his brain. Governed solely
by impulse, and reasoning entirely through the
imagination, he allowed himself first to invent
pernicious and unwholesome theories, and
then with the common fearlessness of mania
proceeded to put them into practice. Byron
simply took the old road of vice, but went
further along that way to everlasting burn-

ing than most other men have dared. Like most vicious men, he felt a morbid pride in boasting of his base exploits, and his vanity enjoyed the reputation of abnormal wickedness, which he had done his best to justify. There is no difficulty in classifying Byron; he was a brilliant rake. But Shelley was an entirely new species, and his place is not yet settled. He held vile views and yet impressed men with a child-like purity. He cursed his father, deceived his friend, and deserted his wife; yet every literary critic for sixty years has hesitated to call him a bad man. His poetry is full of a more subtle and perilous poison even than Byron's; yet its latest editor has declared Shelley one who possessed the qualifications necessary for a saviour of the world.

Was Shelley mad? It seems an insult to suggest such a question, and yet it is not so wholly foolish to do so as may appear. Of course, it would be a monstrous absurdity to suppose Shelley mad in the ordinary signification of the term. The man whose career was one brilliant and orderly development of genius, whose works grew in splendor and magnificence, advancing with sure and steady power, to the very last, was not a man of broken or deranged intellect.   But, nevertheless, a mind may possess the highest qualities and yet miss something of that perfect equipoise which we call sanity.   Christopher Smart was mad, and his stately "Hymn to David" was actually composed while he was an inmate of an asylum.   His madness was local, so to speak, and left his genius free.   He was insane upon certain questions of conduct, but perfectly clear-headed on all other points.   The case is perfectly common, and Shelley does seem, in some points, to approximate to it.   He was mild and gentle until certain subjects were mentioned; then the hectic flush, which Hazlitt noted, appeared, and he shrieked and gesticulated like a dervish.   He approached the most hideous suggestions of moral evil with a smiling nonchalance, and seemed absolutely unconscious that any shame could possibly attach to them.   He had no sense of sin.   The most vicious man shrinks from contemplating certain forms of vice, which to him had no taint of vice about them ; he was as far above such a man in his conduct

as he was below him in his ideas. His wickedness was philosophic wickedness. A man who
was temperate, self-denying, and chaste in his
daily life, in his philosophy of conduct he uttered and propagated ideas which visit the
bulk of men, if at all, as the passing horror of
delirium or madness. He had the madman's
fear of being thought mad. One of his constant illusions was that his father was seeking
to trap him into an asylum, and he declared
that attempts had been made to seize his person. Indeed, the whole history of these illusions—and there were many of them—lends
strong color to the proposition that Shelley
was not a perfectly sane man. A man who
circumstantially describes how his wife has
been wronged, how he has been shot at, how
the officers of an asylum have entered his own
house with orders to carry him off, when there
is absolute evidence that nothing of the kind
ever occurred, and could not have occurred,
would certainly lie under the natural suspicion
of unsound intellect in most societies. That he
also wrote "Laon and Cyntha" would not dis-
pel such a suspicion; indeed, the very manner
in which he advocates, with the most brilliant ·

and alluring genius, immoralities which are not
so much as named among decent men, apparently without the faintest idea that he is
doing any thing criminal or unusual, would
only serve to strengthen the belief.

The question of art and morals is a very
vexed one, and naturally suggests itself in relation to Shelley. One reader, having followed
me so far, will cry out that a man who glorified
incest ought to be drummed out of the regi-
ment of genius, for no splendor of eloquence
or passion of poetry can afford proper apology
for the infamy of his thought. But another
will inevitably reply that Milton advocated
polygamy; and if you are to make men of
genius show a clean bill of moral health, or
sign a self-denying ordinance in regard to aber-
rations of opinion before you admit them to
the temple of fame, in truth your said temple
will remain a very solitary place. You will
have to reckon with the coarseness of Shakespeare, and the bestiality of Swift; you must
convict Coleridge of criminal selfishness;
Lamb's humor occasionally has a distinct
alcoholic flavor; and poor Burns smells so
strongly of whisky, and bears such obvious

traces of the ravages of passion, that no respectable custodian would dream of admitting
him, or even of allowing him to rest within
the porch without remonstrance, or possibly
pious vituperation. That is how it ought to
be, and no doubt would be, if Respectability
had her way, and could always rely upon the
faithfulness of the custodians she might nomi-
nate. She would have burned "Hamlet" together with "Lucrece," with much the same
indiscriminating horror as that of the pious
executor of Wesley, who discovered a much
annotated Shakespeare among the testator's
papers, and hastened to hide from the world
the evidence of such unparalleled backsliding
by consigning his master's manuscripts to the
flames. In fact, we should have had a pretty
regular series of bonfires of the vanities, on a
much more extensive scale than the comparatively humble conflagrations with which Savonarola startled Florence in the fifteenth century. But fortunately, as one might show even
on the ground of morals itself, Respectability
does not exercise the despotism in literature
which she does in drawing-rooms. She gives
her orders with unmistakable precision enough, ·

and doubtless her custodians do their best to
obey them. They make an immense bluster,
as Jeffrey did about Wordsworth, and announce
in stentorian tones that "This wont do."
The Austrian general severely criticised Bonaparte for his intolerable audacity in breaking
every rule of warfare, by fighting battles in the
winter. By every rule of the game the young
man was clearly wrong, yet somehow or other
he contrived to win it. It is so that genius
usually contrives to answer its assailants. The
door-keepers of literature have the very best
intentions, immaculate orthodoxy, alert dogmatism, unlimited pugnacity, profound belief
in their mission, and yet even they hear the
voice of the charmer, charming never so
sweetly, and are beguiled. The music of the
advancing lyre floats like invisible enchantment
on their senses ; its divine cadences might well
make the trees rustle passionate response, or
follow in obedient choirs ; the warders try to
lift their hands to the unswung bolts, but
cannot, for the spell is on them ; they try to
frame the words of ban and doom, but are im-
potent, for a magical surprise holds their lips
dumb, disparted ; and then, without further

parley, from the greenwood bursts the young poet, with eyes aflame and face suffused in rapture, and lightly, as though into a sleeping palace, he leaps the golden threshold, and is seated with his peers in immortal life and reverence. From that secure throne he cannot be dragged down; and though the warders still may suffer much uneasy scruple, yet even they are fascinated, and obliterate the memory of defeat by singing pæans to the victor.

No doubt this perpetual controversy on art and literature is useful to the printer, but it is hard to find any other class of persons who are benefited by it. It is as futile as the endeavor to build houses from the top, and as impossible of demonstration as the squaring of the circle. The plain case appears to amount to this: that men will take their sides on such a question according to the degree in which the æsthetic or the moral sense is developed within them. Like Pilate and Herod, the two may become friends on the day when the human center of their controversy has given up the ghost; but the truce will last no longer than the thick darkness which covers the earth on the day of irreparable loss and mourning. The

disputants are irreconcilable, because they view
their subject from diametrically different stand-
points.   Carlyle would have called Shelley "a
puir creature;" and we have all had an opportunity of learning with what sickening revul-
sion and contempt he read the *Life of Keats*
on its first appearance.   Had Carlyle, then, no
sense of beauty? Few men had a finer.   A
great portion of his writing, and that the noblest portion, is poetry in every thing but the
form.   Not even Wordsworth showed a ten-
derer love of Nature, nor Chaucer a finer fidelity in depicting her, than Carlyle has manifested
in hundreds of rough jottings, sketches at first
hand, which are found in his diaries and letters.   But such passages spring rather from an
unparalleled power of minute observation than
from a keen æsthetic sense. The dominant
stratum of Carlyle's character was morality,
hard Scotch granite, out of which the sweetest
waters could break, and on whose top soil the
tenderest seedlings could thrive—humor, pathos, poetry, the most subduing gentleness, all
were there; but the main formation of his
mind was all the same vehement sternness,
with more than a touch of the Pharisaism that

metes and judges, and swears by the law
rather than the Gospel. He had little love of
music, no love of art, and considerable contempt for any poetry but the poetry of action.
To him it was inconceivable that any human
creature should claim any dignity or reverence
as a minister of the beautiful. Man did not
live to write beautifully—Goldsmith, according
to Johnson, could have done that about a
broomstick—but to act beautifully. When,
therefore, you united in one life the art of
beautiful writing with the habit of infamous
conduct, you presented to Carlyle a monstros-
ity upon which all his bitter ire flamed forth,
and for which his one remedy was instant an-
nihilation. The man of stern moral sense will
always side with Carlyle, and will think in his
heart—some might add, " with the fool "—that
it were better Byron and Shelley had never been
born. The man whose æsthetic sense is strong,
and whose moral sense is weak; to whom
poetry is an exhilaration, and music a passion ;
who can find the most exquisite of joys in a
perfect phrase, and thoughts too deep for tears
in the humblest flower that blows—will always
be ready to pardon any thing to the man who

has baptized him into such delight and wrought
in him such silent rapture. And between
these two parties, who have a creed and believe in it, there will always troop certain dis-
consolate fugitives, who make the old futile
attempt to serve two masters, and perpetually
relieve their troubled consciences by casuistical
papers in the reviews on the relations of morality and art.

Much has been written about the intangibility of Shelley's poetry, but in truth it is no
more intangible than the man. I pause at
this point to consider what is written, and may
make freē confession of certain uncomfortable
qualms. One looks toward that quiet ghost
which rises from the blue waters of Spezzia, or
glides like a sunbeam through the pine forests
of Pisa, or beside the glittering Serchio, and
cries with Marcellus,

> " 'Tis gone !
> We do it wrong, being so majestical,
> To offer it the show of violence."

One might almost add the other lines,

> " For it is, as the air, invulnerable,
> And our vain blows malicious mockery."

Browning asks, " And did you once see Shelley

plain?" as though he too felt that Shelley was
an ethereal presence, a wandering voice, an
Ariel whose life was song, a most complex and
almost intangible personality.   Other poets
have used the pathetic fallacy, and made Nature weep with their grief, and transmute their
joy into bright sunlight and fragrant winds;
but Shelley seems to have sunk himself in
Nature, and made himself the translator of
Nature's mute emotions.   To use one of his
own favorite phrases, his being became "inwoven" with the very life of the universe.
We find it hard to realize him as a bodily presence; he is "as the air, invulnerable."   He
did not live prose and write poetry; he was
poet from the crown of his head to the sole of
his foot; a creature of imagination all compact.   Speaking after the manner of men, we
may doubt his sanity; but we are conscious,
not the less, that our diagnosis has not gone to
the heart of the case and plucked its mystery
out.   It is this remoteness, this insubstantial-
ity of Shelley, which makes it so difficult to
understand him.   We never seem to be at
home with him; just when we have got our
finger on his pulse, and he stoops to whisper

3

his secret to us, a luminous mist falls between us and him, and we see him fade into air, thin air. Sometimes he seems to us a creature of demonic origin, but oftener an eternal child. Has any biographer, Mr. Jeaffreson included, given us the real Shelley yet? To give the real Byron was a very different matter. There a biographer was treading on firm ground, and dealing with flesh and blood; for that matter, with somewhat offensive flesh and blood. But Shelley eludes all human touch. When all the records are gathered into one, when Medwin has blundered, and Hogg has blabbed, and Mr. Jeaffreson disillusionized us; when we have honored his enthusiasm, and pitied his errors, and wondered at his moral obtuseness, and written all sorts of smart and malicious and tender things about him, we somehow feel like the old squire with the French wine, that we have got "no forrader." The voice sings on, in sweet passion and thrilling pathos; it loosens its silver notes and floods us with delight; it is hidden in the clouds, or uttered by the skylark, or lingers in the west wind and the sea; and it sings on as if in supreme contempt for us and our poor judgments, the malicious mockery of our pointless repartee, and stupid cleverness of our mean sarcasms, even as a lark pouring out his soul against the sapphire sky of noontide thinks nothing of the riot and wrong of man, but only of the brightness of the sky and sweetness of the music, and the joy and triumph of life. It is this lack of robust flesh and blood in Shelley which makes both himself and his poetry so difficult of comprehension to the common people. No man has so completely realized the divine fury of the poet, the half-inspired and half-frenzied utterances of the man who is caught up into the seventh heaven, whether in the body or out of the body we cannot tell, and has become the witness of things which it is not lawful for a man to utter. He perpetually produces the impression of visionary splendor beyond all speech ; he strains at the barriers of language till his voice rises in one long, languorous, melodious wail, a lament for impotence, a passionate invocation to the unattainable:

> "Woe is me !
> The wingèd words on which my soul would pierce
> Into the height of love's rare universe,
> Are chains of lead around its flight of fire.
> I pant, I sink, I tremble, I expire."

We listen entranced, as men do to the nightin-
gale, and hold our breath, as the deep mellow
notes bubble forth, and quicken in passion, and
rise in steady flight, higher and yet higher,
clearer and yet clearer, till we can well believe,
when they cease suddenly at the utmost zenith
of rapture, it is because the very throat has
burst, and the very heart broken in excess of
over-mastering ecstasy. Who has read "Epipsy-
chidion" without at least some faint realization
of what this means?   Even Mr. Jeaffreson calls
it the finest love-poem in the universe, and he
is right.   But it is no earthly love ; it is spiritual
passion, the rapture of a soul broken free of
the flesh, but yet using the symbols of fleshly
love, "confused in passion's golden purity." We
pause and think, " He can soar no higher;
mortal speech has done its utmost."   We are
faint and flushed with the difficult air, and can
scarcely breathe.   But Shelley is invigorated,
and again begins, and soars yet higher, and
sings in yet more piercing sweetness, till at last
the sense seems to swoon, and the solid world
slides from beneath our feet, and we, like the
singer, sink and tremble and expire.   When
we wake it is like waking from delirium.   We

have been utterly bewitched in a dream of sensuous beauty, and we rub our eyes to make sure the common earth is still our home. The spell of Shelley has been upon us, and there is no other poet capable of such inimitable magic. But there are few natures that can bear the spell, even as it was a unique nature which produced it, simply because there are many natures capable of pleasure but few of rapture, of pain, but not of agony, for whom indeed, by the necessary limitations of their own character, such words are too divine and deep, and savor more of frenzy than of truth.

To men of an imaginative mind and hard morality Shelley will always appear a mere blasphemous presence. They will never pierce the mist of intangibility and touch the real man. They will find it a congenial task to catalogue his errors and explain the sequence of his sins. What they will not be able to do will be to understand that nature sometimes produces characters of strange complexity, which fall into no category, and touch many classes but belong to none. It is not possible to draw any fixed line between the sheep and the goats at our earthly judgment-seats, or to separate the

wheat from the tares in human character. It
is not possible to label and ticket men, as
phrenologists do the sections of the skull, and
say to precisely what class they shall be rele-
gated. It is difficult even to discern where
virtue grows warped and leans to vice, for the
golden threads are closely bound up with the
stained and blackened ones, and in destroying
one you sometimes spoil the other. Criticism
may be a very excellent employment in the
world of letters, but it is an exceedingly futile
one when it applies itself to character. Most
futile of all employments is it when it approaches
with its yard-measures and compasses a unique
nature, and affects to take its true dimensions
by rule of thumb, and explain its secret with
the offensive glibness of a self-complacency
which is " cock-sure of every thing."

But if to the bulk of men Shelley will never be
a very real presence, or a very lovable one, there
will always be those who will have enough
imaginative insight to discern the real man,
and they will love him with an unfailing devotion. There is no more pathetic figure in
English literature. From first to last he is
solitary and isolated. We see him as a boy, with

eager eyes and bright-flowing hair, alive with fancy, thrilling his sisters and frightening himself by the grotesque visions of an undisciplined imagination ; a frail wild slip of a child, needing more than common children a sympathetic atmosphere, and the kindliest training. But such conditions were utterly denied him. He is the slave of impulse, and with no judgment to regulate that impulse. The benign influence of human goodness, not to say human piety, never fell upon him. The only sort of Christianity he was familiar with was the grotesque distortion embodied in a father whose chief articles of belief were the necessity of orthodoxy and the divine rights of property. The only elderly man who exercised any real influence over his intellectual growth was Dr. Lind, of Eton, and he was an atheist. It is needless to follow the well-remembered details of his expulsion from Oxford, his quarrels with his father, his poverty, his abstinence, his generosity, his misfortunes. It is not wonderful if the original morbid taint in his mind fed upon such food as this, and in his almost frantic love for liberty he advocated license. Life must often have seemed a very sorry business

to him. He never had a public for his writings ; scarcely one of his poems had a sale, and
as he himself says, he wrote for himself and not
for the public. Yet it cannot be doubted he
desired a public, and keenly felt the contrast
between his own literary failures and Byron's
immense success. He tells us in lines of bitter
sweetness :

> "Alas ! I have nor hope, nor health,
>   Nor peace within, nor calm around,
> Nor that content surpassing wealth
>   The sage in meditation found,
>   And walked with inward glory crowned—
> Nor fame, nor power, nor love, nor leisure.
>   Others I see whom these surround :
> Smiling they live and call life pleasure ;
> To me that cup has been dealt in another measure."

Not in that hour of dejection only when he
looked in utter sadness on the bright sea and
purple noon of Naples, but many times did he
feel that he could lie down,

> "Like a tired child,
> And weep away the life of care."

He could not solve the mystery of life—its
shame, its wrong, its anguish ; and like many
another pure and ardent spirit bruised himself in many a wild fluttering against the iron

bars of insolvable problems. And then he
flew to Nature. In her freshness and grandeur,
in the hospitality of her silence, and the friend-
liness of her unchangingness, he took refuge,
and hid himself in her starry pavilion against
the windy tempest of life's futility and malice.
He becomes her high-priest and confidant. He
serves her with unquenchable devotion and
delight. He thirsts for her beauty, and toils
to mirror her glory in fit and perfect speech.
At thirty he is gray-headed, and his face is
lined and furrowed like an old man's. The
spirit of sorrow never leaves him ; his verse is
one long lament, and underneath its utmost
triumph the voice sobs quietly and the sick
heart aches. Then suddenly the end comes,
and Nature weaves her blackest tempest for a
pall and opens the door of rest in the dim
green depths of that unresting ocean he had
loved so well. He dies with purpose, character, and work alike unfinished. We know
what he did, but know not what he might
have done or been. But life is only just begun at thirty, and ended thus in its beginning, surely merits the grace of charity, of
sympathy, of pity. That meed of reverent

feeling has never yet been denied by any
who have drunk of the magic stream of his
poetry, and never will be wanting so long as
English literature endures, and with it the
name of Shelley.

WORDSWORTH AND HIS MESSAGE.

IN the ordinary development of personal culture there are certain usual and well-defined stages. There are voices in literature which appeal especially to youth and rouse its strenuous impulses, and there are voices that do not effectually pierce the soul until the advent of sedater years and the more constant mind. It is seldom that the literary friends of youth are the friends of age, and rare and memorable is that book which casts its glamour over boyhood and has lost no portion of its wizardry in the duller period of fading years. There are few books which have this universal charm, and they are the greatest. They may almost be numbered upon one's fingers, and the names they bear are the peerage of literature.

In that august company Wordsworth cannot be enrolled, for the spell of Wordsworth, exquisite as it is, is limited and very far from commonly felt. Scott is the poet of boyhood, Byron the poet of youth, Shelley the inspira-

tion of early manhood, while to the young
heart Keats is the very minister of sensuous
beauty, the thrilling voice that sings from the
lattices of

> " Magic casements opening on the foam,
> Of perilous seas in faery lands forlorn."

There is a time when the healthy chivalry of
Scott sets the boy's heart thrilling, just as later
the splendid bitterness of Byron quickens it to
revolt, or shadows it with morbid sorrow.
Shelley carries that revolt, as it were, into a
farther world, and fills the firmament with the
same war and passion that Byron breeds upon
the earth. It is the revolutionary note in
Shelley that secures him the ear of youth, and
according to the strength of the poetic fiber in
a youth will he choose either Byron or Shelley as his singer. The shallower nature, or we
might say the grosser nature, will fall a prey
to Byron ; the more spiritual nature will kindle
with the ethereal fury and rebellion of Shelley.
But both, in their measure, will remain over-
mastering influences upon the heart of youth.
Against these Wordsworth has no chance.
There is no fury in his verse. He has no cynicism, no quips and pranks of bitter humor or

bitterer blasphemy. He brings with him no
whirlwind, but a fresh and quiet air; he rises
on us with no tumult of tempestuous clouds,
but with the ineffable serenity and strength of
that "sacred dawn" he loved so well to picture.
He has no brilliance wherewith to dazzle us;
no mystery to fascinate our curiosity, no silent
anguish on his shut lips to move our sympathy.
He is not dramatic; a more undramatic man
never lived. His voice is like the voice of a
ballad-singer following a fantasia; so simple
that we fancy we may scorn it, yet so sweet
and clear that we begin to listen even in spite
of ourselves. The waves of endless storms
break in futile wrath upon the iceberg, but the
warm Gulf-stream comes at last and dissolves
what they could not shatter, and subdues that
which it could never carry by assault. The
influence of Wordsworth upon his time has
been the influence of the Gulf-stream; it has
flowed silently and surely, and has conquered.
It is for reasons like these that Wordsworth
can afford to wait his time. He had to do so
while he lived in relation to his fame; he has
to do so still in relation to his acceptation by
individuals. He wrote for nearly fifty years

amid all but universal scorn, and yet suffered
no diminution of strength or hope, and overcame at last. He will sing in vain still to the
heart of youth full of its first fire and fervor.
He will seem to be a singer of no account, an
aged bard who stands in the market-place and
pipes to those who will not dance. But inevitably there comes a time in the history of any
true personal culture when this quiet bard
draws us to himself, and grapples us with
hooks of steel. He becomes what no other
has become to us—the friend of our solitude,
the inspiration of our duty, the consoler of our
disillusions; keeping full pace with us to what-
soever heights of thought or deed we may as-
pire, and remaining to the end a friend that
sticketh closer than a brother.

It is not to any detailed criticism of the
works of Wordsworth I would now address
myself; the libraries already groan with reams
of disquisition on that subject. Never has
poor mortal been so utterly routed and flouted
as Francis Jeffrey for that famous *obiter dic-
tum* of his, that Wordsworth "wouldn't do."
Among all the unhappy ghosts of hades none
can be much more perennially uncomfortable

than he.   Every fresh cargo of critics ferried
over by Charon for the last fifty years have
brought news of the world-wide fame of the
man who "wouldn't do; " and without doubt,
if they have not forgotten their old urbanity,
they have sought poor Francis out instantly
and given him a piece of their minds.   Flay-
ing a poet must be quite a mild and humane
sport to this posthumous persecution of a king
of critics, as Francis has perhaps discovered to
his cost.   The only question I have to ask
about the poetry of Wordsworth is, What is
the nature of his message to our age?   The
simpler and more interesting question is,
What was the nature of the man himself?

First of all, as regards the man, it may be said
that no one who has written fascinating poetry
has ever had less of the secret of fascination in
himself.   He was destitute of wit, and his attempts at humor in " Peter Bell " are very like
the performances of that celebrated German
baron who thought humor was best attained by
jumping on the table.   He struck most people
as a remarkably prosaic man.   The brilliant con-
versationalists of his day found him dull, and
the Westmoreland peasantry, among whom he

lived, said he was not "lovable in his face, by
no means," and judged from his habitual reticence that he was "a desolate-minded man."
One is tempted to say he lacks individuality, though that would not be true, as we
shall see; but certainly he lacked those dazzling qualities which have made most great
men memorable. There are no enigmas in his
character; he was a simple, just, and temperate man, with no electric flash of wayward passion, no black depth of cynical melancholy in
his nature. In this he is the very opposite of
such a poet as Byron. It is difficult even now
to say whether it is Byron the man or Byron
the poet who exercises the strongest spell over
us. He endears himself by his frailties and
fascinates with his suffering. We think, for
instance, of such a story as that of Lady Caroline Lamb meeting by accident the hearse
that was turning northward with the body of
Byron, and on learning whose it was going
home with a shattered brain, to die; and we
feel, in spite of all juster knowledge, that there
must have been something deep, something
wonderful and fine, in this man's nature that
women should have loved him with such pas-

sionate love. The incident is intensely dramatic, as a hundred incidents in the life of
Byron are, and we are thrilled. That life of
Byron, with its strange speed and splendor, its
swift alternations of brightness and blackness,
its bitterness and baseness and tragic ruin, will
always fascinate mankind. It is a play that
will never tire of studying; it thrills them.
Thus it will happen in the future, as it has
already happened in the past, that the individuality of Byron will preserve his poetry from
decay; the man is more than the poetry. In
the case of Wordsworth the converse is nearer
the truth; the poetry is greater than the man.

This, upon the whole, is the general impression Wordsworth creates, and we simply make
note of it as an impression. It finds further
and amusing corroboration in the general ideas
the Westmoreland peasantry entertained about
him. They felt that, while his qualities were
of the sterling and durable type, yet there was
a total absence of geniality about him. He
did not stop and talk to children; he took his
family out with him for long walks, but usually
went ahead and said nothing to them; he
never laughed and seldom smiled; in fact, "a

4

desolate-minded man." "You might tell from
his face his poetry would never have no laugh
in it," said one of them. "As for his habits he
had noan; niver knew him with a pot in his
hand or a pipe in his mouth," said another.
"He went a-bumming about—bum, bum, bum,
and stop;" "He had a rare deep voice; children sometimes heard it rising in some solitary
place and ran away scared"—are other reminiscences of his habits, or rather, according to
the Westmoreland code of life, his lack of
habits.   It is curious to find how, in their
rough and blundering phrases, these Westmoreland peasants precisely discerned the cardinal defect of Wordsworth's nature—this lack
of geniality and fascination.   Their ideal poet
was poor Hartley Coleridge.   He had very de-
cided habits, and all of the wrong sort; one
fears the greatest part of that sad wasted life
of his was spent with a pipe in his mouth and
a pot in his hand.   But he had this strange
secret of personal fascination: every body
loved him.   His neighbors had great difficulty
in accepting the poetic claims of Wordsworth
—" he was a well-meaning, quiet, dacent man,"
but they believed poor Hartley a very great poet

indeed.   It was commonly supposed that Hartley's relation to Wordsworth was that of the
unfortunate chief to his fortunate subordinate :
he " did the best part of his poems for him,"
so the saying is.   Opinion was slightly divided ;
some thought Dorothy Wordsworth wrote her
brother's poems for him, and some thought
Hartley wrote them, but very few gave Wordsworth himself the credit of them.   In their
way these Westmoreland peasants confessed
that their ideal of a poet was very much akin
to the ideal set up by the morbid school of to-
day ; the poet was a frail wild creature, passionate, fascinating, wayward, addicted to pots
and pipes and other unholy indulgences—
somebody to be pitied by the charitable, hu-
mored by the pitiful, and taken to the heart
and loved forever by the sentimental.   Their
ideal of the poet was the Byronic ideal in fact,
and that is, after all, the prevalent ideal in
middle-class minds ; and Wordsworth, with his
silence, his self-absorption, his love of solitude,
his plain ways and undramatic history, is the
very opposite to this creature of vicious and
unwholesome sentiment.

No doubt the world is very mad and very

foolish, but undoubtedly it sets high store upon this charm of personality of which Wordsworth was so singularly destitute.   It rates it above steadfastness and honor, unsullied probity, untarnished morals.   As a weapon to win fame with it has always proved supreme.   Some of the worst of men have been the idols of the people by simple virtue of their power of fascination.   Probably no two men ever lived with harder, narrower, more intensely selfish natures than Bonaparte or Charles II., but see how they fascinated men ! The old gray cloak and cocked hat of Bonaparte were followed by the adoration of millions; their appearance before a hostile city was sufficient to make every soldier drop his arms and cry, " Vive Napoleon ! " and before their magical approach a throne tottered and a kingdom relented. Charles II. was as shallow and graceless a scamp as ever sullied the name of prince, but men poured gold into his lap when he smiled, and forgot the Dutch fires blazing at Sheerness when he jested.   The very gigantic nature of the wickedness of such men has been a source of fame, an element of success ; for men admire great sinners almost as much as they do

great saints. It is vain to appeal to the Byron-
Lytton school on behalf of Wordsworth.
Against these giaours and corsairs, these gentlemen whose melancholy is permanent and
attractive, who reduce seduction to a science
and elevate despair into a fine art, these Cag-
liostros of poetry, who are most brilliant when
most wicked and increasingly famous as they
are increasingly depraved, William Wordsworth
has no chance. Men like to be dazzled, and
Wordsworth holds no such spell ; he is not
histrionic, he is not melancholy, he is not
wicked ; and the public which desires such
qualities in a poet will always hold the " quiet,
dacent man " of Rydal Mount in vast contempt.

It might very well be shown that this Byronic ideal of the poet is not merely false, but
is new. It was a fashion that came in with the
Revolution, for nothing was more shaken in
that wild whirl of tumult than the moral con-
victions of men. One can find no trace of this
diseased sentimentalism in the four greatest of
all poets—Homer, Dante, Shakespeare, and
Milton. The peculiar virtue of Wordsworth is
that amid all that breaking up of laws and
customs he kept his sobriety, his serenity, and

his faith. He fell back upon the essential facts
of the universe, and felt that, though all king-
doms were shaken, there was a kingdom that
must remain. His theory of poetry was the
conscious · or unconscious outcome of that
calm conviction. What was that theory? Put
in its briefest form it amounted to this : that
it was time for poets to return to nature, to
natural and simple themes, and to clothe such
themes in the plain language of the common
people. It asserted the dignity of common life
and the sacredness of the natural affections.
It was a protest against the diseased sentiment, the histrionic melancholy, the faithless
cynicism which had corrupted the life of English poetry, not less than a protest against the
meretricious glitter of the style in which such
poetry had been couched. His poetry was
meant to be a rebuke against a debased poetic
style, and his character and career were yet a
finer rebuke against a debased poetic life.

Added to this, Wordsworth claimed for
poetry a religious mission, and invested it with
the sanctity of a divine calling. The long
critical warfare waged against the Lakers was
not fought out upon the comparatively triv-

ial issue of pure or ornate style; it touched
far deeper and more essential questions.   The
poet was in his eyes a high-priest, and his art
was a ministration.   This was not a new idea
in poetry; it had already been asserted in the
splendid and energetic eloquence of Milton.
It is curious to notice that not even in Shakespeare, and still less in Homer, is there any
trace of this idea.   In what are probably the
last lines Shakespeare ever wrote—the epilogue
to the " Tempest "—when, like Prospero's, his
charms were " all o'erthrown," he especially
defines his conception of his work, when he
says his art is to enchant, his project is to
please ; though he does indeed strike a note
of more solemn and pathetic significance when
he adds :

> " And my ending is despair,
> Unless I be relieved by prayer."

But apart from this mere hint at the diviner
height and aspect of his art he gives no sign.
In Milton alone, among the peers of earlier
English poetry, does this conception of the
poet's art find its full expression.   But with
Milton the idea has a rigidness and limitation
which are not found in Wordsworth.   In Milton

it exhales the flavor of the noblest Puritanism;
in Wordsworth it is of wider application, and
includes the noble paganism of lofty nature-
worship.   The poet with him is again a seer,
an interpreter, a speaker of the deep things of
God; but he is more: he is a natural man,
whose days are bound together by natural
piety, and whose spirit is lost in deep com-
munion with the spirit of the living universe.
He serves before the everlasting altars of the
high mountains, and has passed into the holiest
place of the mystery of universal life.   His
whole attitude is priestly; the world is a living
temple roofed with splendor, and he has in his
gift absolution and peace for the souls of erring
men.   He is no mere ephemeral person; he is
in the great apostolic succession of truth, and
his diocese is as wide as the walls of heaven.

Let any one weigh such lofty claims as these
against the sensational cynicism of Byron, or
the light tintinnabulation of Mr. Thomas
Moore, and the uniqueness of Wordsworth's
position in the dawn of the nineteenth century
will be at once apparent.   While all the poets
of his day were ransacking earth and heaven
for some new form of sensationalism, and were

busy blowing bubbles of brilliant froth in the
heated chambers of society, he had taken refuge in the serenity and strength of nature,
and had found thoughts too deep for tears in
the humblest flowers that blew. · While they
were swept along the wild mill-race of revolution, or whirled in the worse vortex of personal
or social debasement, he had stepped aside into
the clear light and solemn solitude of the everlasting hills, and heard the broken thunder of
the mad world only like a distant undertone,
too distant to be terrible, but near enough to
bear witness to the tragic heart of life—" the
still sad music of humanity."   While their
ideal of a poet was a miserable and misan-
thropic being, whose book was written within
and without with mourning and lamentation
and woe, Wordsworth had formulated his idea
of a poet thus—and the sketch is obviously a
portrait:

> "But who is this with modest looks
>   And clad in sober russet gown?
> He murmurs by the running brooks
>   A music sweeter than their own;
> He is retired as noontide dew
>   Or fountain in a noonday grove."

What an apparition is that for the curled

darlings of the Byronic school to gaze upon!
It is Chaucer, shorn of his humor and turned
philosopher; it is Thomas à Kempis, worshiping Nature and changed to poet! What wonder that grave face and russet gown became
merely a target for ridicule amid the profligate
glitter of the regency? What marvel that a
world which was going mad over the conjugal
infelicities of Byron had scant attention for a
man who brought them the crystal water of
simple joys rather than the delirious cup of
passion, and sung of running brooks rather
than the diseased secrets of an unhappy life?
We do not ask nowaday which is the truer
ideal of the true poet. The world has left
Byron and come round to Wordsworth. It is
enough to remember that the final achievement of the one is "Don Juan;" of the other,
"The Excursion."

Lovers of sensationalism will of course turn
from Wordsworth to the end of the story; but
that is simply evidence of their own shame
and his glory. The select souls are given to
the singer with the russet gown. It must be
owned that the poet finds what he brings: the
sheep know his voice, and the voice of a

stranger do they not know. Wordsworth knew this truth, and thus it was he had so large a faith in time and so sublime a confidence in himself. To every man of genius the veiled angel of destiny makes offer of two caskets and bids him choose. The one glitters with jewels and is ablaze with gold, but it is empty. The other is plain and undecorated, but it endures when jewels are scattered and gold lost in the miry roads along which the weary armies of mankind march, and it is full of the suffrages of posterity. The first casket is the prize of immediate notoriety; the second is the pledge of enduring fame. Many there are who choose the first, and few are they who trust their deeper instincts and choose the second. Of those few we know now, though sixty years ago none suspected it, that William Wordsworth was one; and this was the victory that overcame the world, even his faith.

We have noted some of the sterner features of Wordsworth's nature which rendered him unattractive—his self-absorption, his reticence, his lack of geniality—but it is quite possible to construct, from the broken hints that have

come down to us, a picture of the real Wordsworth which is as beautiful as it is true. What
a tender picture that is, for instance, which one
of the old female servants of Rydal Mount
draws of him humming the lines of a poem,
while " Miss Dorothy kept close behint him,
and she picked up the bits as he let 'em fall,
and took 'em down, and put 'em together on
paper for him." Dorothy Wordsworth is one
of the most memorable figures in literary history, and deserves more than passing mention.
It was she who met her brother when he returned from France, with broken hopes, after
the terror of the Revolution, and led him back
to Nature, and taught him to attain that calm
insight which is the bliss of solitude. Her
greatness, and it is the divinest greatness, lay,
like Mrs. Carlyle's, in her self-renunciation ;
she was content to minister to her brother's
genius and to find her chief joy in the growth
of his mind. The love of the lake district was
hers before it was his, and it was she who
transmitted and fostered the passion in him.
How many a touch of felicitous energy or tender truth she added to his poems we have no
means of knowing; but we cannot help sus-

pecting that it was she, and not Mrs. Wordsworth, who added those two most exquisite
lines to the poem of the Daffodils:

> "They flash upon that inward eye
> Which is the bliss of solitude."

Never had poet more fit companion for his
lonely walks than Wordsworth had in this
woman, who knew what sociality there is in
silence, and never broke it with vain words,
and knew even better what suggestiveness
there is in heartfelt speech, and never spoke
save to gather up in memorable phrase the
rare and fleeting sensations of visionary beauty.
The two most memorable literary companion-
ships of the first half of this century were
those between Charles and Mary Lamb and
William and Dorothy Wordsworth. The ineffable pathos of the one is as lovely as the
calm and simple sentiment of the other. If
there is yet a great artist left among us who
desires two national themes for two immortal
pictures here are the subjects to his hand.
For the first picture let him seize that moment
when Charles and Mary Lamb cross the last
meadow on the way to the asylum ; the pale,
stooping scholar hand-in-hand with the strange,

dark-eyed girl—both weeping, both weighed
down with an intolerable secret, both pilgrims
on the Via Dolorosa of infinite sacrifice and
sorrow, each clinging to the other with despairing love and the anguish of foreboding fear.
For the second let him paint the tall figure of
Wordsworth, with the "round blue cloak and
big wide-awake, poorly dressed at the best of
times," followed closely, at the distance of
half a pace or so, by Dorothy Wordsworth,
with her eager face and clear eyes—busy not-
ing in her book the last stanza of such a poem
as "She dwelt beside the banks of Dove,"
while round both rise the mountains, checkered
by the April drift of light and shade, and in
the near distance lies the tarn of Further Gow-
barrow, beneath the shadow of whose shore
there gleam that

> "Host of golden daffodils
> Beside the lake, beneath the trees,
> Fluttering and dancing in the breeze."

In one picture there would live the tragic anguish of life ; in the other, its solemn ecstasy.
In both there would be represented immortal
love.

Quite as fine in their way are other pictures

that might be drawn of the real Wordsworth. Every one will remember his description of the love of skating, and how, hissing along the polished ice,

> " Not seldom from the uproar he retired
> Into a silent bay, or sportively
> Glanced sideway, leaving the tumultuous throng,
> To cut across the reflex of a star." .

What a fine picture that would make! The clear black ice of one of the lonelier mountain tarns, the winter sparkle of the stars, the solemn peaks buttressing the blue and windless vault of heaven, the distant cry of some solitary night-bird, and the long vibrating ring of the lonely skater—for sounds can be hinted at in a great picture and interpreted by the subtle process of true art to the imagination—and that lonely skater, flying like a winged shadow hither and thither, the poet who has made those solitudes his home, and has dedicated his life to the interpretation of their mystery. The only word that strikes like false art in the description is that word "sportively." We are quite sure in such a scene Wordsworth would be touched to solemnity rather than sportiveness. In such a moment a mind like

his would have kindled not so much with the
exhilaration of the sport as with the weird
beauty of the scene. His thought would be
of the swift rush and mystery of life, the im-
mensities that lie beneath it and above it, life
itself seeming but "a troubled moment in the
being of the everlasting silence." Given star-
lit midnight, and a belt of darkened mountains,
and we have the two great natural agencies
best able to produce solemn and searching
thoughts in the heart of man. It is a scene
in which the ode on "Intimations of Immor-
tality from Recollections of Childhood" might
have been conceived. It was a scene, as he
himself has reminded us, in which he recognized "a grandeur in the beatings of the
heart," and felt the power of that

> "Wisdom, and spirit of the universe !
> Thou soul, that art the eternity of thought !
> And giv'st to forms and images a breath
> And everlasting motion !"

I think, of all the many pictures full of
simple grace and beautiful serenity which
crowd upon the memory from the writings of
Wordsworth, there is none I would so readily
choose as a fit and noble setting for a true

portrait of him who has taught us more than
any other

> " How exquisitely the individual mind to the external
>   world
> Is fitted, and how exquisitely, too,
> The external world is fitted to the mind."

Certainly there has been not merely no more
memorable figure in modern literature than
William Wordsworth, but no more memorable
figure in relation to modern life itself. Many
men feel in the first enthusiasm of youth that
they have a mission to fulfill, but few men have
the courage and fidelity to pursue their mission. " The world is too much with them ; "
they are speedily seduced by its fascinations,
and enslaved by the overmastering force of its
conventionality. Wordsworth found his mission when he went to dwell among the lakes,
and he was heroically faithful to it through evil
and through good report. He turned aside
from the race for honor and place, not with the
spiteful cynicism of disappointment or the
bitter passion of contempt, but in obedience
to the mandate of a serious and simple spirit.
Few things in literary history are more striking
than the retirement of Carlyle to the desolate

5

isolation of Craigenputtock; but Carlyle's retirement was limited in time and imperfect in
renunciation. In his heart he never ceased to
covet the fuller and more passionate life of
cities, and felt that Craigenputtock was a
prison. It is, perhaps, all the more powerful
testimony to the strength of his unique character that he bore so great and painful an im-
prisonment of gigantic energies for so long.
But he never fully acquiesced in his severance
from more social life. He never regarded it
as final; he never thought of it otherwise than
as a means to an end. When Wordsworth
turned his face northward he broke the last
bond that linked him to conventional life, and
he did it willingly. He knew that he was going to live as a peasant among peasants, and
he was content. He meant to dedicate his
great powers to a task that might be hopeless, that must be prolonged, that could not
be other than hard and sacrificial in most of
its conditions; but he did it, and never re-
gretted it. In later days prosperity dawned
upon him; but very few have clearly understood what the world would call the "hard-
ships" of those earlier days. If ever "high

thinking and plain living" found not merely
an apostle, but an example, it was in him.

To the readers of to-day the old ideal of
poetry in a garret has become an obsolete
fiction. *Our* poets live in palaces ; they are
connoisseurs and patrons of art ; they flit with
the easy grace of wealth from country mansion
to town-house ; they no longer haunt the
patron's gate.   Do they not sit cheek by jowl
with Dives?   Have they not even been known
to descend to the peerage?   And do they not
receive yearly checks that run into the dignity of four figures?

But Wordsworth was "a mean-living man,"
as the peasants say, living even more simply
than they.   "Never wore a boxer in his life,"
said another—always the round cloak and plain
raiment of the peasant.   When he rode abroad
—we regret to mention so impolite a circumstance, but Mr. Rawnsley* says his neighbors
all aver it—it was in a dung-cart, with a board
across and a bit of clean bracken at the bottom.
His library had no choice editions or delicate

---

* Mr. Rawnsley is the author of an excellent paper on the
"Reminiscences of Wordsworth among the Peasantry," printed in the *Transactions of the Wordsworth Society*. I am much
indebted to him, and hereby acknowledge my obligation.

bindings; it was plain and scanty. In every
feature of his life this austerity of habit is visible. He had set himself to teach how few are
the real wants of man; how deep and divine
are those common joys of the affections which
are within the reach of all; how self-sufficing is
simplicity; how false and fevered is the life of
man when it is withdrawn from the healing influences of nature and degraded into a wild
scramble for the soiled gold or tinsel glory of
ambition; and that which he taught he practiced.
"We know only what we practice," was his
motto, as well as Savonarola's. The well-spring
of his philosophy was in the order of his own
life. That life thus became the finest sermon
ever preached to this hurried age of ours, the
finest and the most needful; and its divine
lesson was:

> "What an empire we inherit,
> As natural beings in the strength of nature."

When we justly consider these things I
think we shall find a new William Wordsworth emerging from the shadows of the past,
and surely not an unlovable Wordsworth. We
shall forget his awkwardness and stiffness in
those brilliant circles of society which he

visited now and again in the days of his late-
dawning fame.   We shall forgive him that his
poetry has so little of passion in it, and upon
the whole we shall be thankful for it.   There
are many other poets who can give us passion ;
but who else can give us peace?   To whom
can we go so well in the hour when our hearts
are grieved and our nerves worn down by the
ceaseless harass of life amid a crowd?   I do
not say when our hearts are broken ; for then
we ask for a teacher who has himself passed
into the sanctuary of sorrow, and trodden the
wine-press alone, and Wordsworth cannot claim
to have done that.   It may be true, as Matthew
Arnold has exquisitely put it, that

> " Wordsworth's eyes avert their ken
>   From half of human fate ;"

but that is only saying that Wordsworth has
the defects of his qualities.   But who else presents the same qualities and ministers to us
the same "sweet calm?"   And even in the
hour of sorrow such serenity as his is sometimes even more welcome than the sympathy
of others.   It is, in fact, a nobler sort of sympathy—calm, godlike, healing.   Not in vain, and
not with sacrilegious arrogance, did he esteem

his art a ministration ; in the oldest and truest
sense the minstrel and the minister are one, and
such minstrelsy is his. He ministers to the
mind diseased, and his medicine has the wholesome potency of nature. He brings the freshness of the mountain air in his presence, and
his voice is like the lark's. We love him as we
do that winged " pilgrim of eternity," and we
can listen to him when all other songs distress
our jaded sense. Who has not fled from his
Babel, vexed, troubled, worn out, and in the
blessed solitude of Nature felt his strength
renewed while he stood amid the open fields
and clothed himself with their silence as with
a garment, and felt again the breath of blue
sky over him and heard again the magic
whisper of the leaves and brooks? Wordsworth has so perfectly absorbed that charm of
Nature that his poetry does for us just what
Nature herself does in such hours as these : he
purges and refreshes us. If poetry is, as some
one has beautifully described it, the Sabbath
influence of literature, Wordsworth breathes
upon us the very Sabbath of poetry—its rest,
its devotion, and its healing calm.

Certain it is, no English poet has shown so

perfect a fidelity in his descriptions of Nature.
He may claim to have set a new fashion in
regard to her—the fashion of minute and exquisite observation.   His life was essentially
an out-door life, and that is the secret of the
perennial freshness of his charm.   Nothing escaped those vigilant eyes of his; and his sense
of sound was as perfect as his power of vision.
This wonderful precision finds an admirable
example—the best that I can think of—in
that terse and perfect picture which he gives
of the desolate, windy height of a lonely
mountain pass:

> " The single sheep, and that one blasted tree,
> And the bleak music of that old stone walL"

He was, moreover, what the peasants called
"a verra practical-eyed man."   He hated to
see the slightest wrong inflicted on a landscape by the stupid folly of man.   He used
his authority to secure the right building of
chimneys and in the prevention of the vulgar
use of colors.   When a copse was cleared the
dalesman would leave a few trees standing
that his eye might not be offended.   He insti-
tuted himself by common consent guardian of
that beautiful district which he had learned to

love so passionately, and he taught the dales-
men to take new pride and pleasure in its
preservation. This also was part of his mission, and not an inglorious part; and for this,
too, I love him. In those long walks of his
he was guarding and securing one of the
choicest heritages of the English people; and
all who are still left among that people, who do
not bow down and worship before the omnipo-
tence of the railroad, and whose chief aim is
not to spin a little faster than their neighbors
in the wild dervish-whirl of vulgar ostentation,
will thank God for William Wordsworth, and
thank William Wordsworth for what he did.

The gift, then, that Wordsworth brings to
us is serenity, and the message he delivers is
simplicity. We do not go to him to be excited but to be strengthened. He, in his turn,
does not pose before us in a dramatic attitude,
as a suppliant for sentimental pity; he stands
before us as a wise teacher, in whose lips are
the words of everlasting life. Those who do
not love him must revere him; but, for my
part, I find it easy to do both. If poetry be
something more than a pool of chaotic sentiment, that gives forth iridescent vapors, brill-

iant films and bubbles; if it be a healing
stream, flowing clear as crystal from the
throne of God and bordered by the trees of
life; if it be an inspired voice, "a vision and a
faculty divine," then in Wordsworth I recognize the noblest poet of our century. "This
wont do!"   O, Francis Jeffrey! had you but
known it, this man spake the words that made
for your peace and ours; he brought precisely
what would do, the book bitter in the lips to
critics like you, but sweet and healing to the
soul of our vexed, tumultuous generation;
the one medicine, the one message that we
most imperatively needed.   It is precisely
such ministration as this that our age needs
still; and our house of literature will be left to
us desolate indeed when such sweet voices
shall have died out of it.   What he meant to
do, and what he did, Wordsworth has severely
defined for us in four memorable lines:

> " The moving accident is not my trade,
>   To freeze the blood I have no ready arts;
> 'Tis my delight alone in summer shade
>   To pipe a simple song to thinking hearts."

"The moving accident "—no; for it was
Wordsworth's creed that life is not determined

by its accidents but by its essence, and that
its divinest possessions are its simplest and its
widest characteristics and emotions. The freez-
ing of the blood—no; for sensationalism is a
base and easy trick—the trade of the necro-
mancer, but not the function of the poet; it is
his to make sunlight in a shady place; to call
men back to their inalienable heritage of natural joys; to visit them with gifts of benedic-
tion and of peace; to teach them the secret of
divine tranquillity in a life freed from haste
and lifted high above the unholiness of ava-
rice—

" To pipe a simple song to thinking hearts."

RELIGIOUS DOUBT AND MODERN POETRY.

MATTHEW ARNOLD, BROWNING, TENNYSON.

MR. W. E. H. LECKY, in his learned *History of European Morals*, has commented, in a striking foot-note, upon the immense growth and influence of the newspaper press, and on the fact that it is chiefly directed by lawyers and barristers. Mr. Lecky's inference from the last-named circumstance is that a "judicial" tone is thus introduced into the daily press, and a "judicial" method of thought consequently imparted to the public mind. From this inference we totally disagree; for the lawyer-barrister mind is essentially forensic, not judicial; and one very general issue of newspaper press influence upon the public mind is political and social partisanship. A far more important result of the enormous growth of the press is the great impetus given to the taste for reading among

the classes to whom at one time literature of
any kind was a sealed and sworded paradise,
whose trees of good and evil were jealously
guarded against the encroachments of the
multitude and the curiosity of the vulgar.   At
the present moment it may almost be said
that the flaming swords wherewith intolerant
and exclusive legislation used to guard the
garden have burned themselves out, and the
great domain, with its crowded and accumulated growth, lies open, without toll or hin-
derance, to the poorest.   Therein are to be
found trees of knowledge as stately as Milton's,
and founts of song as pure and deep as Wordsworth's; but the face of Villon leers in the
shadows, and the pestilent obscenity of Con-
greve, Sterne, and Swift has left many a livid
pool of poison on the verges of the greenest
lawns and at the roots of the mightiest forest-
growths of genius.   In a word, such freedom
brings its natural peril, and the wayfarer finds
the serpent close beside the tree of knowledge
still.

Not merely has the reading public increased,
but, as a natural consequence, the writing public has also steadily grown.

" The mob of gentlemen who write with ease " was never so large as in the present day. There is a vast number of minds endowed with a mimetic gift which passes for a literary instinct, and education and opportunity conspire to kindle a literary ardor which finds its vent in books that benefit nobody but the trunk-maker, and between whose birth and oblivion there is but a step. The mass of so-called poetry which is published, and which actually commands attention and numbers its editions, is what Dominie Sampson might well call " prodigious." Much of this successful verse is the product of fine and cultured minds who find in verse-making one of the many pleasant and most easily acquired arts of literature. Much of it succeeds by following the reigning fashion or by modeling its " silvery see-saw of sibilants " upon the method of the latest favorite ; much more is simply the ludicrous contortion of ambitious mediocrity, and its whole vocation is endless and very indifferent imitation ; and therefore it is a question of the highest importance, Who and what manner of models are the poets thus set up as examples ? Voltaire's barber hastened to assure

his master that he did not believe in God any
more than the gentleman did; and it is certain, in poetry as in every thing else, that the
master-mind finds itself mimicked and echoed
in every particular by the inferior. If the master sing of Chloe and Phyllis, straightway the
chorus will sing in hundred-fold laudation of
Daphne and Sylvander; if of blessed damosels
and anguished lilies, the chorus multiplies its
dirges of faded sunflowers and its raptures at
the moving vision of blue china; and if the
master degrade his genius to chant the blas-
phemies of atheism and the swinish revels of
carnality, the chorus will sing in yet grosser
fashion the democratic upheaval and the apotheosis of the brute.

Moreover, it must be remembered that the
chief ministry of poetry is a ministry of suggestion. The poet is the interpreter, but not
the less the leader, of his age. His words may
not become the street-song of the multitude
or the solace of the poor man's hearth, but
often a higher and more strenuous fate is
theirs—they become the inspiration of the
thinker. The influence of a great poet on the
best minds of his generation is like the action

of the sunlight ; silently it gathers force and spreads itself abroad and marks the fullness of its power by the ripened bloom upon the fruit and the depth of tint and color in the flower. In like manner the highest prose-genius of a time often takes its color from the highest poetry of the period. Often the poet is content to leave his exposition in the hands of the few whom he can trust, knowing well that through the influence of those few his words will not fail of reaching the widest audience of his time.

Therefore, if it be said that the great bulk of the people do not read poetry, we can only retort that every writer for the press in this country does ; that the leaders of opinion on every great social and religious question do ; that the poet first molds the fervid mind of youth in our public schools, and overshadows our universities with his presence, and meets us in Protean fashion in every avenue of our common literature. Civilization has advanced, but as yet we have not seen any sign of the fulfillment of Macaulay's prophecy in the decline of poetry. At the crest of the far-rolling wave of civilization will always be found the

highest outcome of the poet's "vision and
faculty divine." Civilization, so far from destroying poetry, has really done very much to
intensify it; but it has changed its methods.
It has robbed poetry of the old freshness and
simplicity of its utterance, the ancient force
and directness of its form, and has surcharged
it instead with the feverishness and satiety of a
complex modern life, full of many aims, throb-
bing with the pulse of large and eager purpose, and saddened by the vain pursuit of a
perfect culture, which more and more proves
itself an unattainable and mocking dream. So
long as the human heart remains poetry will
not die nor the poet's mandate be withdrawn.
Man never yet has lived alone upon the bread
which the wealthiest civilizations have kneaded
for his use; nor will any "ethics of the dust,"
any applications of a marvelous science that
merely multiplies the conveniences of social
life, or claims his curious wonder at the price
of the denial of his religious instincts, suffice
him now any better than heretofore. Pascal
long since reminded us of the undying truth
that "the heart has reasons which reason does
not know," and poetry may be described as

the reason of the heart. And it is because we feel that our higher culture will rather indorse and widen the poet's mandate than abridge it that we think there can be no more serious problem presented to the investigation of the thinker, in the interests of the society of the future, than the problem which seeks to measure and define the influence of our modern poetry.

Let it be granted, then, that a distinct new note, or rather series of new notes, has been struck in the poetry of the last fifty years, the distinctive characteristic of which is the problem of religious faith.

The supreme question of the present day is the attitude of the age toward religion, and that question finds a hundred reflexes and vain solutions in our poetic art. Of course, it may be said the century opened with the fierce strife of religious doubt and denial in the poetry of Byron and Shelley, and that, therefore, this is no distinctly new feature of our latter-day poets. But there are many respects in which Byron and Shelley differ wholly in their attitude toward religion from their lineal descendants in poetic art. It was said of

6

Byron by Shelley that unfortunately he could
not help believing in a hell ; and this statement
admirably illustrates his habitual conduct in
dealing with matters of faith and piety.   His
libertinism was ingrained, his infidelity was an
affectation.   When he is throwing his wildest
doubts into the air he never loses self-con-
sciousness ; he has his eye upon the gallery,
and waits for its applause.   He is so ill an
actor that whenever he strikes an attitude he
pauses to measure its effect.   Whatever he says
against his beliefs he cannot help believing ;
and one cannot help feeling that he writes
profanity in much the same spirit in which he
talked of his desire to know the sensations of
a murderer merely that he might enjoy the
childish pleasure of watching the horror he
was certain to excite.   Shelley's atheism, on
the contrary, is undoubtedly sincere.   But it is
rather the frenzied scream of an excited boy
than the iconoclastic fury of a full-grown man.
It is not merely rebellion against orthodox
faiths, it is wild and unmeasured revolt against
every form of use and order which tradition
sanctions.   And how different this is from the
sad wail of our modern agnostic poetry must

appear in the hastiest comparison.   The key-
note, the very ground-tone of such poetry, is
poignant and unavailing regret.   It touches its
deepest and most pathetic chords in dirges and
lamentings, in farewells to the dying faiths and
requiems for the dead.   The air is full of such
notes of sorrow, the tremblings of unmistakable distress, the vague and wild vibrations of
a woe too deep for words.   Its very sadness is
its fascination, for to many minds the holding
of a doubt seems a vastly finer thing than
the holding of a creed.   And although it
must be distinctly acknowledged that doubt,
like other things, may become a fashion,
and poetic doubt may be the mere affectation of an affectation, yet it may be admit-
ted that the bulk of our agnostic poetry is
too evidently sincere:

> " A fever in the pages burns
>   Beneath the calm they feign ;
> A wounded human spirit turns
>   Here, on its bed of pain."

And it is this very sincerity which makes it so
formidable and forcible an influence in mold-
ing the age.   Sincerity and sadness, welded
together in high poetic achievement, must in

any age of the world win hearing and alle-
giance; for is it not too common a characteristic of the race itself, full of unsatisfied desires
and instincts as it is, to listen rather to "the
still, sad music of humanity" than to the voice
that sings good cheer?

Every generalization has its exceptions, and
there are exceptions here. The old revolutionary note of Byron and Shelley still vibrates, and the old revolutionary hope still
burns. But for the most part we have grown
too familiar with revolutions to expect any
swift or bright millennium from the noblest
of conspirators or the most magnanimous of
patriots.

Mr. Swinburne still hurls Byronic defiance,
and cherishes the hope of Shelley; he leaps
upon the altar he has made, and when he can
withdraw himself from singing in the Les-
bian orgies chants before the face of Baal in
democratic odes and vituperative sonnets.
But he stands alone. The latter poetic movement has scarcely heart enough for joining in
any song so strenuous; it is saddened with its
disillusions; it is satiated with its gains; it is
emasculated in its energies, and what offensive

power it has left is mainly spent in small sneers against the tyranny of creeds and sympathetic lamentation over the decay of ancient faiths and pieties.

The culmination of this spirit of sincere and saddened doubt is found in the poetry of Matthew Arnold, and a very brief analysis of a very small portion of his writings is sufficient to indicate its scope and character. He has described himself as

> " Wandering between two worlds, one dead,
> The other powerless to be born,"

as an exiled Greek on some far northern strand, thinking of his own gods,

> " In pity and mournful awe might stand
> Before some fallen Runic stone ;
> For both were faiths, and both are gone."

It must be a matter of somber gratification to the poet to know that the critical public has generally consented to accept him at his own estimate, and that he is described as a modern Greek oftener than by any other phrase ; just as Goethe is rightly described as a modern pagan. But between the Hellenism of Goethe

and that of Matthew Arnold there are wide dif-
ferences. A great critic has described Goethe's
Hellenism as " the completeness and serenity
of a watchful, exigent intellectualism ; " and
Matthew Arnold's expressed admiration for
"the wide and luminous view of Goethe"
leads us to infer that there might be no description he would more earnestly covet or
endeavor to deserve. But Goethe's paganism
is simply indifferent to all forms of modern
faith, and is without moral predilection, while
Arnold's is full of wistfulness and yearning.
The mission which Arnold has to proclaim is,
that with the best desires and intentions toward belief, unfortunately he cannot believe.
So far from being a modern pagan he has described in lines of great strength and beauty
precisely where the cardinal failure and corrup-
tion of ancient paganism lay :

> " On that hard pagan world disgust
>   And secret loathing fell;
> Deep weariness and sated lust
>   Made human life a hell.
>
> " Stout was its arm; each thew and bone
>   Seemed puissant and alive,
> But, ah ! its heart, its heart was stone,
>   And so it could not thrive."

He looks with wistful rapture backward to the hour of the first victories of the Christian faith, and cries:

> "O, had I lived in that great day,
>   How had its glory new
> Filled earth and heaven, and caught away
>   My ravished spirit too!"

It is, perhaps, unnecessary to remark that he who will not believe "Moses and the prophets" is not likely to believe even if "one rose from the dead." The poet who sings agnosticism in the nineteenth century would probably have sung any thing but Te Deums in the first. Still, it is of painful interest to note how faith, so long repressed, bursts forth into momentary triumphant assertion, and cleaves to the Crucified when the cross is removed to the second century. What cannot be done in a modern England corrupted by "beer-shops" and "dissent," * what it is impossible to accomplish with the eyes of Strauss upon us, and agnostic reviews around us, might perhaps have been attempted in that dim be-

---

* In his eloquent article on "Isaiah of Jerusalem" in the *Nineteenth Century*, Mr. Matthew Arnold, in enumerating the "hinderances with which religion in this country has to contend," places at the head of the list, "beer-shops, Dissent!"

ginning of years, when at least the great de-
lusion was new and beautiful :

> "No thoughts that to the world belong
>   Had stood against the wave
> Of love which set so deep and strong
>   From Christ's then open grave.

> "No lonely life had passed too slow,
>   When I could hourly scan
> Upon his cross, with head sunk low,
>   That nailed, thorn-crownèd man."

Yet in the poetry of Matthew Arnold faith is
but an artistic freak. The voice of modern
denial speedily re-affirms :

> "Now He is dead !   Far hence he lies
>   In the lone Syrian town ;
> And on his grave, with shining eyes
>   The Syrian stars look down."

There is nothing left for it but to toil on in
a waste and weary world full of "forts of
folly" manned by coarse . Philistines, or to
"let the long contention cease," and, like the
kings of modern thought, be dumb: "silent—
the best are silent now." Some vague and
visionary religion of humanity may still be
possible :

> " He only lives in the world's life
>   Who hath renounced his own."

Some vaguer pantheism may perchance explain the future ; in the last hour let not needless priest nor friend be near ; but rather let the poet look forth from the open window on " the wide aerial landscape bathed in the sacred dews of morn," and rejoice to know he will speedily be absorbed in " the pure eternal course of life," and be one with that he gazes on.   For his father he shall sing the noblest of dirges, for he was one of the strong souls who led the wavering lines of humanity

> " On to the bound of the waste,
>   On to the city of God,"

and stood in the end of the day like a good shepherd with his flock in his hand.   But the son is one of those who comes at last to the inn of death alone, and is barely saved out of the peril in which so many comrades have fallen.   Surely there can be no more desolate intellectual outlook than this, and it is not surprising that it is the source of the most mournful poetry.

This is by no means the place to discuss the actual condition of the Christian faith, and did we dare to dissent from the verdict which Matthew Arnold and his school have returned

against it we should no doubt be immediately
catechized as Philistines who are blind to facts,
and as optimists who are what they are because they are ignorant.   But we may at least
be permitted to remark that religious doubt
and modern poetry appear to have united
themselves in a most unhappy marriage, and
are in their most fascinating guise but an ill-
assorted couple.   The greatest treasures of our
English poetry are the product of an age of
faith, and were scarcely possible without some
wise and deep belief.   It was in an age when
religion was the paramount subject in English
politics and national thought that Spenser and
Shakespeare flourished; it was at the conclusion of the greatest war for conscience' sake
which any nation has known, and by the pen
of a man who more than any other embodied
in his own person the stern and holy ardors of
the period, that our greatest epic poem was
- produced; and amid all the loud thunder
of the Revolution-time Wordsworth's spirit
caught the first rising music of the new age
of faith, and that new age of faith fitly inspired
his serene and pious strain.   The fact is, religious faith is inextricably interwoven with

our English poetry; it has given it fullness and serenity, and it will secure it permanence. We have never yet written "Crush the Infamous" upon the banners of our literature; we have never clothed a harlot in the garb of Reason and called her goddess; we have never yet consented, and never shall consent, to the monstrous modern theory that art can know no morals. We have been spared the demoralization of many alternate tyrannies and revolutions, and so surely has our ordered freedom grown out of our religious life that we may well believe there is some force in hereditary ideas which must ever make a faithless poetry foreign to the English mind. Folk-lore tells us how it is an ancient superstition that mandrakes when torn from the ground shriek in their every root and fiber like dumb living things driven into sudden speech by anguish. May we not apply the fable and declare that poetry dragged from its immemorial rooting in the soil of faith shrieks aloud and becomes a thing of anguish and despair? It is a fatal experiment; it will not and it cannot come to good. It is too late to try to turn the tide of English literature; it has set too long upon

the sunny shores of faith to ebb at last toward
the icy solitudes of apostolic indifference and
despair.   The English mind will never yield a
wide attention to any modern Lucretius in the
person of a Matthew Arnold, singing his despairing ode concerning "The Nature of
Things;" and still less will it "dance to the
piping of an educated satyr" in the person of
Mr. Swinburne.

Indeed, the more the matter is considered
the more evident does it become that religious
doubt has exercised nothing but a destructive
influence on English poetry.   Edgar Allan
Poe, in one of the most weird and wonderful
of his extraordinary stories, pictures a per-
plexed and noble genius in the act of suicide.
As the clock strikes, and the clear day shines
into the perfumed and splendid chamber, the
suicide lifts a costly crystal goblet to his lips
and pledges his last hour in the fatal draught.
When the drained chalice is set down again,
behold it is cracked and blackened.   In like
manner our modern genius sits in garish misery and fills the crystal cup of poesy, which
should be for the healing of the nations, with
its poison-draught of doubt; but when the cup

is set down again it is cracked and blackened. It is not wholly destroyed; but it is hopelessly disfigured by the base uses to which the unworthy put it. To use a choice and beautiful Venetian goblet to hold the black draught of acrid poison is no greater prostitution than to make poetry, which is the handmaiden of faith, minister to denial. If the light that is within the poet be darkness "how great is that darkness!" The very spring of thought is broken, the very light of song is quenched; the poet is like a pianist who plays with one hand and on few notes; more than half the chords are dumb, and the full compass of the instrument he can never reach.

Let any student rise from the perusal of such poetry as that which A. H. Clough has written and say whether this be not the real impression made upon his mind. Here is undoubted faculty for song; but this note may not be struck, for it is too high; nor this, for it is too divinely deep; and so the poet veils his face, and his voice is heard only in faint whispers and warring thoughts and wailings of an infinite distress. The poet can " only soar in one direction," it has been said; but if the

blue heavens be closed and unattainable what
else can he do other than limp along the common earth, with trailing wings and wounded
heart, pouring out the sad wild notes of an
irremediable woe?

It may of course be said that Tennyson and
Browning, incomparably the two greatest poets
of our time, have in nowise stood aside from
the great controversy of disputed faiths, and
that their poetry nevertheless is marked by
majestic strength and the noblest artistic completeness.   Indeed, in both poets we have distinct and splendid poems wholly devoted to
the discussion of moral and religious doubt.
In such poems as " Easter Day " and " Christ-
mas Eve" Browning may be said to have
hunted certain forms of skepticism home to
their

> " Inmost room
> With lens and scalpel "

of the most acute and brilliant analysis.   And
in poems like " The Two Voices," " The Palace
of Art," and above all the " In Memoriam,"
which stands in unassailable fame above all
comparison, Tennyson has wrestled with the
toughest doubts that have strained the thews

and sinews of the mind since the day when
Socrates,

> " Fired with burning faith in God and right,
> Doubted men's doubts away."

But it must at once appear that the discussion of doubt is a very different thing from the
profession of denial. Life will never cease to
be mysterious, and while life is full of mystery
doubt will never cease. A gray under-roof of
mystery shuts us down ; a deep sea of mystery
moans and thunders at our feet. There are
awful moments of eclipse through which the
strongest spirit may be called to pass ; sorrows
come upon us not alone, but in companies, and
sweep all before them ; we move for a while
amid such starless desolation, and such waves
and billows have passed over us, that it may
well happen that our feet have almost slipped.

Let the Book of Job serve us for an illustration. The great drama of the trial of Job
opens with the scene of Job worshiping in the
very moment when the last messenger has
reached him with the bitterest of all his evil
tidings ; and it closes with the victory of faith,
with the patriarch once more worshiping, so
that the latter end of Job is more blessed than

his beginning. Now, throughout the history doubt is only stated as the foil to faith; it falls with the blackness of eclipse for a little space, but obeys the law of the eclipse and vanishes at last, leaving the sun shining in his strength. It is precisely in this spirit that both Tennyson and Browning deal with the problems of religious doubt. There are two voices, but the triumph of the great argument does not remain with the mocking voice. There is a "vision of sin," but its black and bitter cynicism dies at last in a faint, mysterious dawning splendor; and though the divine voice speaks in a tongue no man can understand, yet its final utterance is on the side of hope. In the "In Memoriam" we have the dense thunder-cloud, and even the rolling of the thunder, but there comes at last a season of clear shining, when a serene and holy light fills earth and heaven. The great chords of wailing die away, one by one, into the murmurous joy of infinite hallelujahs; the purposes of loss are seen, the chastening of bereavement is achieved, the wine of sorrow has been drunk, the heavens of song are purged and clear, and in their unfathomable depths there gleam the dimly outlined walls of the city where He dwells who has made all things new, and where those lost from earth have larger life and holier knowledge.   It is true some "bitter notes" his harp has given, but

> "Hope has never lost its youth."

> "If e'er when faith had fall'n asleep
> I heard a voice, 'Believe no more,'
> And heard an ever-breaking shore
> That tumbled in the godless deep;

> "A warmth within the heart would melt
> The freezing reason's colder part,
> And like a man in wrath the heart
> Stood up and answered, 'I have felt.'"

The reason of the heart has proved itself victor over the reason of the intellect, for it was diviner.   Wailings in the night there may have been, and cryings after light, amid blind clamor and doubt and fear—

> "Then was I as a child that cries,
> But crying, knows his father near;"

and in the light of this great spiritual victory the whole problem of the tangled world grows clear; the world is safe in God's hands, and already there are prophetic signs and heraldings of its full redemption—

> "That one far-off divine event
> To which the whole creation moves."

7

Not less unmistakably has Robert Browning
declared himself a singer upon the side of faith.
He is a stronger and deeper man than Tennyson; an incompleter artist, but a greater poet;
and his method of approaching doubt wholly
differs from Tennyson's. He loves to assault
it with sardonic humor, to undermine it with
subtle suggestion, even to break out into grim
laughter as it slowly disintegrates and falls into
a cloud of dust before his victorious analysis.
But not the less does he sympathize with whatever there may be of spiritual yearning, of
earnest but baffled purpose in it; and no
poet has ever been quicker than he to place in
the fullest light of tender recognition the one
redeeming quality there may be latent in the
thing he hates. For faith, in Robert Browning, is a spiritual fire that never burns low.
Through whatever labyrinth of guilt or passion
he may lead his readers, God is ever the attend-
ing presence, in whose hands all the ravelled
skeins of life lie distinct and clear:

> " He glows above,
> With scarce an intervention, presses close and palpitatingly."

Human life is lived out in every instance
beneath the eye of God, and it is the failure to

recognize this which is the beginning of all evils in human character. The lightning which startles the guilty lovers hidden in the deep forest is in truth God's sword, plunged again and again through the thick cloud to find them, for they cannot flee from him; and the prison-roof of life that shuts the mourner in will assuredly break some day, and "heaven beam overhead." Whenever Browning walks amid the shadows of human mystery—and darker glooms no poet has moved through—he sees the star of faith shining overhead, he hears the voice of God bidding him be of good cheer. David, as he sings in the black tent before Saul, bids him think of his mother held up on her death-bed, and bids him again

> " Hear her faint tongue
> Joining in while it could to the witness,
> ' Let one more attest
> I have lived, seen God's hand through a life-time, and all was
> for best.' "

Little Pippa, as she passes out for her brief holiday, her light feet moving innocent amid all the crime and tragedy of life, sings:

> " The year's at the spring,
> Morning's at seven,
> The hill-side's dew-pearled ;
> God's in his heaven,—
> All's right with the world."

It is the poet's own soul that sings in little
Pippa ; this faith of his that all is right never
deserts him.   He will discuss doubt, but as a
strong man who has overcome it ; he will admit
it to his temple of song, but he sternly relegates
it to its own place, and will allow it no supremacy.   Indeed, it is not too much to say that
the greatness of Robert Browning as a poet is
in no small measure due to his greatness as a
believer.

The first direct result of the presence of
doubt in modern poetry is found in that note
of weariness and sadness by which it is distin-
guished.   Its household gods are too clearly
shattered ; it is beside the waters of Babylon
the poet sits and sings.   We do not by any
means seek to prove that the element of sadness which we find in all exquisite poetry in-
variably owes its origin to loss of faith, for no
conclusion could be more falsely partial.   Perhaps the noblest pages in the literature of all
nations are the saddest.   The spirit of Dante
moves between infinite light and gloom, wear-
ing ever a crown of sharpest sorrow ; the majestic woe of the blind and aged Milton has
not yet ceased to thrill upon the world's ear ;

even the serene genius of Wordsworth finds thoughts that " lie too deep for tears." Earthly life is so full of incompletion, is so often baffled in its highest purposes, is so often mocked in the moment of its sublimest yearnings, and has so many chapters in its book of years steeped in deepest pathos that it may well be

> " Our sweetest songs are those
> That tell of saddest thought."

But then life is not wholly sorrowful, and the poetry misjudges life which interprets it alone by tears. Dante has his beatific vision, his " Paradiso " following close upon his " Purgatory ; " and out of the great blackness and desertion of that blind old age of Milton rises the sublime " cathedral music " of his " Paradise Lost " and the hopeful closing vision of his " Paradise Regained." The exquisite sadness of regret, of memory, of vanished hopes and broken fellowships, will ever be one of the noblest elements in any noble poetry.

But all this is very different from that *personal* note of weariness and sad dissatisfaction which is heard so loudly in our later poetry. The greater poets write little of themselves ; the lesser modern poets write of little but

themselves. Their chief inspiration is too frequently a sort of cynical melancholy. They
have been disillusioned; there is nothing new
and nothing true—and no matter! The most
morbid introspection is interwoven with the
saddest worldly wisdom. Few of them, indeed,
are there who

> " Do but sing because they must,
>   And pipe but as the linnet sings."

What Matthew Arnold has called the " lyrical cry" is genuinely heard ever and again,
but too often, while the weariness is sincere
enough, the verse falls into spasmodic affecta-
tions. We feel while we read that there is no
" natural piety " linking day to day in the lives
of such poets. The fresh and clear delights of
Nature are obscured; the cheerful gospels of
the singing birds and sunny day are dumb;
life is bred upon a hotbed of morbid thought,
is passed in feverish turbulence, or creeps on
" wounded wing," and the poetry which expresses it is a melodious spasm or a fitful and
exceeding bitter cry. How can it be otherwise
when the divine aspects of life are blotted
out? What bird can sing in full-throated ease
beneath a threatening thunder-cloud? Faith

has ever been the inspiration of the grandest
human heroisms, the noblest human thoughts;
what wonder that the clew of life is lost when
faith is lost?   Simplicity has always been the
crown of highest genius; what marvel is it
that when the simple heart is lost the whole
world of thought falls into mournful bewilder-
ment and weariness?   There are many pages
in Tennyson which teach us how dangerous it
is even for the strongest nature to drink long
and deeply of the bitter draught of doubt,
how even the final faith of later days cannot
wholly heal the old wounds that still " ache
and cry."

A second result from loss of faith in our
modern poetry is the undisguised and contam-
inating sensuality which has latterly infected
it.   In both Tennyson and Browning we meet
every-where a profound moral sense.   In the
poem of " The Palace of Art " we have a distinct and memorable sermon preached upon
the world-old text that the noblest culture and
the purest art become destroying forces when
divorced from moral fervor ; that even when
unstained by any breath of baser passion they
end inevitably in isolation and despair and

the broken-hearted cry of " All is vanity." The
need of some diviner salvation than art can
offer haunts with persistent bitterness the human
spirit sheltered in its selfish splendor ; at last it
falls, like Herod, " struck through with pangs
of hell ; " it is on fire within and howls aloud,

> " What is it that will take away my sin,
> And save me lest I die ? "

The " Palace of Art " is a sermon for which
the age owes Lord Tennyson profound gratitude.   How much it is needed we can judge
when we remember how often of late years we
have heard high critical authorities insisting
that art must be loved for art's sake, and that
our common notions of morality are wholly
opposed to art.   We could forgive Mr. Swinburne the frantic sound and fury of his revolutionary odes, but we cannot forgive him
when he prostitutes his noble gifts to uphold
the monstrous thesis that the priceliest poetry
is that which deals in the prurient details of
" fleshly fever " and " amorous malady."   The
laureate calls upon *his* soul to

> " Arise and fly
> The reeling Faun, the sensual feast ;
> Move upward, working out the beast,
> And let the ape and tiger die."

But it is precisely in the filthy carnival of
"ape and tiger" that Mr. Swinburne has
chosen to sport. The whole subject is one
which will not bear handling, and, for our part,
we have no desire to publish any investigations
in putrescence. Such poetry can only be la-
beled as "unfit for human consumption."
Certain of its admirers have ventured to call it
"Greek;" but it is not Greek, it is simply
bestial. It is the lowest and most revolting
phase of the evil wrought in literature through
lack of faith. That lack of faith inevitably
leads to such a depth of moral fall we do not
say, but we do say that such poetry is in itself
an awful illustration of how swiftly godless art
may become immoral art.

Here, then, we may fitly close this fragment-
ary study of one phase in modern English
poetry. It is a phase which must be full of
sad suggestion alike to the philosophic thinker
and the Christian. The fatal *narrowing* tendency which attends the intellectual processes
of skepticism is nowhere seen in a more startling light than in its action upon poetry. The
freshness and spontaneity of song is lost, the
lyrical cry becomes a lyrical wail, simplicity

and fullness of emotion become unknown, and
the imagination, having lost courage for any
thing like colossal effort, is frittered away and
wastes itself in spasmodic and often morbid
creation. There is no clearer lesson taught us
by the history of human thought and action
than that the greatest deed and utterance are
impossible without the serenity and courage
which spring from living faith in God. There
is no compensation for the loss of faith in
poetry. Doubt may sometimes lift its cup full
of the wine of misery to the poet's lips, and
he shall drink and find a certain bitter exhilaration in the draught which fires the mind
with brief poetic *fervor*, but that throb of
short and daring effort is all too dearly purchased. The world asks that its poets shall be
prophets, that its singers shall be believers,
that their inspiration shall be drawn from
above, else it were better that their gift died
in them and their song were never sung.

The key-stone in the arch of life is God; if
once the poet pluck that down what wonder
is it that all his life falls straightway into illimitable despair and ruin? What wonder that
the stars fade one by one above him, until at

last he sits in cities of dreadful night and bows his head, and only asks to die? In poetry, as in philosophy, it is needful to insist upon the abiding power and presence of the religious instinct. All outrage done to that is outrage upon that which is noblest in humanity. It brings its revenges with it, and the Nemesis which follows skepticism in poetry is confusion and paralysis of power and effort. Nor is it possible, as Tennyson has shown us, for any man to be even indifferent to the religious instinct and yet be a great poet. It is not given to the mightiest genius to

"Sit as god holding no form of creed,
But contemplating all."

In attempting to shun the most solemn problems of the universe, and work out for himself a perfect intellectual culture, such a poet simply builds a palace of art, whose splendid corridors ring at last with his despair, and all whose glory he is glad to barter for a cottage in the vale where he may mourn and pray. The religious instincts of the race have always been the secret springs which have led the great poetry of the world; and the iconoclast who would propose to himself the daring programme of eliminating faith in God from the poetic literature of England would speed-ily discover that his proposition meant the de-struction of every thing which the common consent of four centuries has voted best worth preserving.

From Robert Browning we may take one line which should be the first article in any poet's creed:

"Earth changes, but thy soul and God stand sure."

From the verse of him "who uttered noth-ing base," we may quote what seems to us as beautiful a conception of the poet as poet ever uttered, and one which our generation were wise in laying to heart: the true poet is

"One in whom persuasion and belief
Have ripened into faith, and faith become
A passionate intuition."

HENRY WADSWORTH LONGFELLOW.

THE death of the poet Longfellow removed a familiar name from the roll of
living celebrities, painfully reminding us how
fast the giants of our generation are falling.
The round table of the Victorian age of fame
shows many empty seats, and there are already
significant signs that the old order changeth,
yielding place to new.   The foremost workers
and thinkers of our day are old men, to many
of whom the award of fame has come tardily,
and from whom little more victorious achievement can be hoped for.   The perfect work of
a poet is usually that of his middle-manhood,
and as seldom that of his latest as of his earliest years.   America cannot expect any further
important contribution to her literature from
the serene genius of the inheritor of Longfellow's fame, J. Greenleaf Whittier, the " Her-
mit of Amesbury ; " and we must confess that
neither England nor America has given any
sign at present of a great poet who is likely to
succeed to the throne of a Tennyson or a

Browning, a Longfellow or a Whittier. In
the moment of common loss, when the master-
hand falls into the long sloth of death, and the
work is fresh with the final touches of its
"cunning," it may be said we are not likely to
form a just estimate of the powers of a de-
parted poet, such as future ages will indorse.
We can, however, seek to form some proxi-
mate idea of the value of the legacy be-
queathed to us; and it is both a graceful and
fitting thing that the hour of death should be
the signal for such a task.

The outward landmarks of the life of Longfellow are few, and call for no special notice.
He was fortunate enough to obtain a profes-
sorship of modern languages in Bowdoin
College, Brunswick, at the age of twenty, ex-
changing it six years later for a similar post in
Harvard College, Cambridge, where he succeeded Mr. George Ticknor. This post he
held until 1854, when he retired to the quiet
country house where his last labors were com-
pleted and his last hours spent. He more
than once traveled widely on the continent of
Europe, leaving the beaten pathways of the
mere tourist and seeking the still waters and

green pastures of national life and character in
its rural solitudes.   On his last visit to England, in 1868, he was received with accla-
mation and awarded honorary degrees by both
the ancient universities.

His life was singularly tranquil, though not
unvisited by those sadder of God's angels,
against whom, as he reminds us, the strongest
cannot close the door, and the best would not
if they dared.   It was never his lot to be the
target of controversy or the by-word of the
slanderer; no foul-lipped or malicious criticism
has vexed the poet's soul; on the contrary,
his claim as a poet has been heartily acknowledged from the first, and his fame has been
wide and constantly increasing.   When we remember the long and painful struggles of
many of our older poets for standing-room and
hearing, and the slow and doubting recognition
awarded to our most famous living poets, it
should surely be accounted a happy thing that
there were quick ears in the world to catch the
earliest song of this singer, and generous
hearts to welcome and applaud it.   Immediate
space to work, sincere and ungrudging praise,
a life of quiet literary toil, serenity and growth

of intellect, length of days, an old age full of
honor, and the mourning of two continents—
all this reads like a young poet's idyllic dream
of life rather than the narration of prosaic facts.

Longfellow had reached the comparatively
stable age of thirty-two when his first modest
volume of original poems, *Voices of the Night*,
was given to the public.   It is no detraction
from his great merit to infer that his power of
self-restraint must have been enormous, or
that he was wanting in the impetuous fire of
temperament which has marked the development of some of the world's greatest poets.
At the age when Longfellow launched his first
skiff of song upon the wandering sea of opinion
Burns and Byron had produced their finest
work, and at even an earlier period Keats and
Shelley had written all that the world can judge
them by.   Probably something may be traced
to both the above suggestive clauses.   Longfellow has himself reminded us:

> " Art is long, and time is fleeting,
>   And our hearts, though stout and brave,
> Still, like muffled drums, are beating
>   Funeral marches to the grave."

His lofty conceptions of the dignity of his
art would not permit him hastily to challenge

the verdict of the public ; least of all by any
thing crude in form or unpolished in expression.   The attentive student of English poetry
will have observed among the foremost signs
of our own times an exactitude of expression,
a delicacy and subtleness of phrase, and a degree of reserve and suggestiveness in the
poetry of his own generation which may almost be taken as its distinguishing quality.
We do not mean that the older poets of the
century display no suggestiveness and finish
of phrase, because this is one of the most
marked accomplishments of all true poets,
and of none in higher degree than Shakespeare.
But in the older poets the apt and splendid
phrase seems to leap into being without effort,
while in the younger it is manifestly the result of patient, and even painful, effort.   On
the one hand, we cannot but admire the con-
summate patience which holds back the poetic
genius until the fermenting crudities of youth
have worked themselves clear ; and we recognize the result in poems which are as perfect in
form as they are chaste and polished in expression.   On the other hand, we miss the Titanic
power that bursts the bondage of form, creating
8

for itself new types in the unhewn granite of
its own originality. The truly great artist
obeys, but is unconscious of his art.

> " He does but sing because he must,
> And pipes but as the linnets sing."

It is pretty sure to follow that the young wings
will dare the ether before their strength is perfect, and will droop, and even fail disastrously;
but it often follows that at last they soar into
a vaster heaven, whose heights and depths remain forever closed to spirits less daring.

And in truth Longfellow has always shown
a nice discernment of the limitation of his
own powers, and has not invited failure by attempting too much. It is mere nonsense that
assigns to any genius the illimitable; every
artist has boundaries which he may not cross,
and the truer the artist the more carefully does
he abstain from any truant raid into another's
kingdom. Longfellow has carefully marked
out the frontiers of his domain, and within
these he has moved with ease as undisputed
lord. He is pre-eminently the poet of the
household and the affections. He has never
indulged in the slanderous wail of the pam-
phleteering or poetic pessimist; and still

less has he pandered to the obscene delirium
of those modern singers whose heritage of infamy it is to have founded what is termed
"the fleshly school."   He has sung of virtue
and manliness, of self-restraint and self-sacrifice, the dignity of labor, and the hidden purposes of suffering.   He is not unconscious of
the sealed enigmas of life which have no perfect answer here ; he does not stifle those solemn questionings which moan like an unquiet
wind through the chambers of the heart in the
darker moments of experience and thought ;
but neither does he coquet with doubt or
probe the mystery with morbid interest and
sensational result.   A genial wisdom, a health-
ful cheerfulness, a living faith in God's goodness and the wisdom of his purposes, pervade
his pages; and of the harder riddles of this
life he has learned to say :

> " Let us be patient!   These severe afflictions
>   Not from the ground arise;
> But oftentimes celestial benedictions
>   Assume this dark disguise.
>
> " We see but dimly through the mist and vapors,
>   Amid these earthly damps :
> What seem to us but sad, funereal tapers
>   May be heaven's distant lamps."

It is no lowly gift which enables a human
soul to sing forth in imperishable words the
sacred joys and sorrows of domestic life.   The
world needs many poets to keep the fountains
of emotion fresh with the sweet troubling of
sympathy and sentiment; but the poets of
the hearth and household are needed more
than any.   Such poets may not quicken the
impulses of intellectual life, but they do as
needful and as great a work; they purify the
atmosphere of the emotions and sweeten the
brackish waters of earthly discipline.   We are
told in the preface of one of the latest and
most beautiful of the innumerable editions of
Longfellow's poems that the publishers have
found Longfellow more in request than any
poet save Shakespeare.   Of course any attempt
to draw a parallel between Shakespeare and
Longfellow would be simply absurd.   But men
cannot help asking on what is such an enormous popularity based?   If any poet, not a
hymnist, be found upon the cottage tables of
our artisans, and in the humble homes of our
peasantry, that poet is likelier to be Longfellow than any other; and there are probably
thousands of persons, not habitual students of

literature, though otherwise well-informed and
intelligent, who scarcely know whether Longfellow was an Englishman or an American.

What marvelous combination of splendid
faculties has conspired to make this man the
most widely-read poet of two hemispheres of
English-speaking people? The probable answer is found in the household character, the
tender, Christian spirit of his poetry. Moreover, he is easily read. There are no obscure
passages, which might be construed backward
as intelligibly as forward. His verse is limpid
as a running brook, and as full of music; it
glorifies, but does not drown the thought. He
writes in clear, strong, nervous English; and
his lines have the power of clinging to the
memory. Few men have already told a story
in verse with a more simple directness, and
in lines so compact and ringing. And this
is the sort of poetry by which the universal
heart is always won. The scholar loves the
veiled meaning underlying classic form; the
intellectual reader ponders on the subtle
beauty, the shadowy and suggestive grace of
lines that fascinate by their very indefiniteness
of outline; but the heart of the people will

always turn to the troubadour, the story-teller, the man whose clear and simple thought chooses for the raiment the clearest and simplest language. It is half a fashion in the present day to admire obscurity, and value a poet according to the number of utterly incoherent and contradictory meanings which may be extracted from any given line. In the face of such a fashion, which a coterie would fain persuade us is the higher criticism, it is well to remember that the most popular poet of our own day is one of the most lucid of English writers, and owes his popularity in no small degree to the definite directness of his style.

The great need in criticism is breadth and sanity; the power to distinguish justly the thing that is good after its kind upon its own merits; and the great danger in criticism is bigotry, subservience to the tyranny of an isolated and perhaps false theory. Thus the reproach against Longfellow, that he is commonplace, is founded upon his manifest lack of certain qualities which constitute the greatness of his contemporaries. But because he has not the mellow and sometimes over-ripe sweetness of Tennyson, nor the subtlety

of Browning, it is not fair to forget that he has
certain gifts of his own which are not to be
despised.   A cameo may be as fine a work of
art as a painting crowded with the angels of
Fra Angelico ; and the song of a thrush in the
fresh glory of an April morning may throb
with as real and beautiful a music as a great
organ " trumpeting " melodious thunder " from
its golden lips."   The place that Longfellow
claims is the place of a singer in the great temple, and if his voice has not the resonant volume
of the great masters, it has the delightful flute-
like freshness of the choir-boy's unspoiled alto.

We have pointed out the absence of creative
originality in his poetry ; and we confess that
the artistic error which most easily besets him
is the proneness to moralize, appending to
every simple song of thought or action its ap-
propriate lesson, as the moral is appended to
the fable.   But all that this proves is that he
is debarred from equality with the great creative poets ; and it does not invalidate his right
to a place as honorable, if not as high, among
the second rank of poets.   Longfellow has
suffered from the very vastness of his popularity.   He is read in the days of youth ; and

books that are read too early are apt to be forgotten in the later and maturer years of life.
Defoe and Bunyan build up their gleaming
wonderland round the steps of childhood,
and for that very reason are seldom re-read,
until the distracted taste, wearied with novelty
and surfeited with the feverish brilliancy of
modern styles, is glad to turn again in the
evening of life to the immortal pages which
made the marvel and the heaven of life's morning.   The common and almost inevitable result
is that such masterpieces are underrated; and
this has been the penalty of Longfellow's
enormous popularity with the young.   But let
the reader take up again the pages so familiar
to his boyhood, and let him include in his sur-
vey the maturer works of the poet, and he will
probably be astonished at the sweetness and
grace, the power and inspiration, of poems
which he read in the holiday moments of a
school-boy's life or in the idle interval between
school and business.

What, then, are the special qualities by
which Longfellow will be known in the days to
come, and by the authority of which he may
claim the bays of the accepted poet?

His greatest claim to the seat of earthly fame
will undoubtedly be that he is the first truly
American poet.   But such a statement has important reservations, which must be remembered before it can be discussed.   It will have
escaped no one that a very large number of
Longfellow's poems are cast in mediæval
molds.   He lingers lovingly over the parch-
ment scroll written thickly with the fancies of
the days of yore ; he is familiar with " the great
cloister's stillness and seclusion ; " he watches
with a sympathetic eye the patient monk working amid the dusk on the emblazoned page,
and praying while he works,

> " Take it, Lord, and let it be
> As something I have done for thee."

He has adopted many a quaint turn of monkish fancy, and is at home with the weird won-
ders of monkish superstition.   And few poets
have translated from the songs and ballads of
other nations so largely as he.   Admirable and
scholarly translations from the French, German, Spanish, Swedish, and Norwegian languages are scattered thickly through his works,
while Dante has absorbed his constant attention and has found in him a clear and truth-

ful interpreter.   But when we have made these
important reservations, when we have glanced
over the long list of translations, the poems
with foreign titles and full of foreign yearnings,
the ballads drawn from the histories of all nations, and bearing in their every fiber the stamp
of the Old World inspiration, the fact remains
that Longfellow is the author of the three most
distinctively American poems in the world.
In one of the interludes to the " Tales of a Way-
side Inn," when the "long murmur of applause" had died away—

> " ' These tales you tell are one and all
> Of the Old World,' the poet said,
> ' Flowers gathered from a crumbling wall,
> Dead leaves that rustle as they fall ;
> Let me present you in their stead
> Something of our New England earth,
> A tale which, though of no great worth,
> Has still its merit, that it yields
> A certain freshness of the fields,
> A sweetness as of home-made bread.' "

This is precisely what Longfellow has done for
the poetry of his country. Any English writer
with equal gifts, living in any English county,
might have written the measured verse of
Bryant, or the serious poems of Lowell, or the
bulk of the poetry of Whittier ; but no purely

English writer could have composed " Miles
Standish," " Evangeline," or " Hiawatha."

It has been said that America has every
thing but a past. Longfellow has shown that
his country is not deficient even in this item
of national wealth by successfully unsealing
the fountains of her early Puritan history and
weaving into the original cadences of one of
the longest poems of the century the strange
dreams and gospels of her ancient Indian
mythology. " Hiawatha " exhales the very
fragrance of the broad prairie and illimitable
forest, and is steeped in an atmosphere pecul-
iarly and perfectly its own ; " Evangeline," the
" tale of Acadie," presents a lovely picture of
the idyllic side of Puritan existence, its sweet
homeliness, its purity and faith, its restrained
but tremulous and intense passion ; " Miles
Standish " is a rougher transcript of Puritan
life, but equally perfect in verisimilitude and
suppressed humor ; and each poem is one
which the world will not willingly let die.
Whatever vast advances the literature of America may make in the future—and we have the
right to expect a marvelous development in
the literature of a nation so young, so strong,

so fertile in resource and eager in invention—
we may safely prophesy that these three poems
will never sink into obscurity. They are three
great landmarks in the advancement of American history which can never be wholly sub-
merged.   And if " Hiawatha " and " Miles
Standish " in any future age attract the attention only of the antiquary or the critical student of his country's literature, " Evangeline "
will share the nobler fate of a sympathetic
welcome from all ages capable of understanding a great poem whose highest charm is simplicity, and especially in that land where its
writer lived and died, and from whose past its
history is drawn.

We have not space for any elaborate analysis of the purely literary characteristics of
Longfellow ; it is rather to the high moral
value of his writings that we would draw attention.   But these literary characteristics may
be briefly indicated.   Those who accuse Longfellow of mere prettiness of phrase and com-
monplaceness of design must be singularly
blind to the exquisite fancy which is found in
all his work, and not infrequently the rare
power of a vivid and minute imagination.   In

such sea-songs as "The Wreck of the Hesperus," "The Phantom Ship," and especially the "Ballad of Carmilhan," we detect the true master's touch, the high and rare power of painting a perfect picture in perfect words. It would be hard to discover ten simple lines which describe the bursting of a storm at sea more perfectly than these from the last-mentioned poem :

> "Eight bells ! and suddenly abaft
>   With a great rush of rain,
> Making the ocean white with spume,
> In darkness like the day of doom,
>   On came the hurricane.
>
> "The lightning flashed from cloud to cloud,
>   And tore the dark in two ;
> A jagged flame, a single jet
> Of white fire, like a bayonet,
>   That pierced his eyeballs through."

So in the ballad of "Scanderbeg" there are lines terse, powerful, and ringing, as ballad lines should be, and instinct with the same quality of casting into clear relief the bodiless vision of the mind. And where there is not the higher triumph of imagination there is always the delicate filagree-work of a pure and tender fancy. Many an exquisite line, and

more than one perfect lyric, has been written
on the lark, but Longfellow's lines may still be
uttered with delight :

> " Up soared the lark into the air,
> A shaft of song, a wingèd prayer,
> As if a soul, released from pain,
> Were flying back to heaven again."

Sometimes this power of fancy runs into
quaintness, as when he speaks of the cares of
the day folding their tents like the Arabs, and
as silently stealing away; and sometimes it
approaches the grotesque, as when he speaks
of the moon shining on the snow which covers
a poet's grave, and the broad sheet of snow

> " Written o'er
> With shadows cruciform of leafless trees,
> As once the winding-sheet of Saladin
> With chapters of the Koran."

But far oftener the fancy casts light upon the
facets of some simple image, and causes them
to glow with a serene spiritual beauty, as in
the musings of the abbot in " The Golden
Legend : "

> " Slowly, slowly up the wall
> Steals the sunshine, steals the shade.
>
> .   .   .   .   .   .
>
> Upward steals the life of man
> As the sunshine from the wall.

From the wall into the sky,
From the roof along the spire ;
Ah ! the souls of those that die
Are but sunbeams lifted higher."

It is needless to quote where every retentive memory can supply its favorite example. There is scarcely a poem which does not manifest the same delicate power of admirable fancy, if not of fervid imagination.

And it would be still more impertinent to quote examples of the sweetness and pathos which have made so many of Longfellow's poems household words. How many hearts have thrilled to the subduing pathos of the lines :

" There is no flock, however watched and tended,
    But one dead lamb is there ;
There is no fireside, howsoe'er defended,
    But has one vacant chair !"

How many aged eyes have looked upon the forms of little children with the same instinctive forecast of the future which Longfellow expresses in such lines as these :

"O little feet ! that such long years
Must wander on through hopes and fears,
Must ache and bleed beneath your load ;
    I, nearer to the wayside inn,
    Where toil shall end and rest begin,
Am weary, thinking of your road !"

It is one of the distinctive charms of Longfellow that he is the children's poet ; the fresh
grace, the agile hope, the dew-like purity of
the child's heart and mind perpetually fascinate
him.   More than once he takes a little child
and sets him in the midst of the world's feverish circle, preaching by the child's innocence
the highest of all lessons.   To say that the
conception and thought of such poems as
" Resignation " is what any average man of
sentiment might feel is not to depreciate them,
but to confer the highest praise.   It is virtually
to acknowledge the supremacy of the poet by
confessing that he has interpreted in melodious
verse and with just appreciation the sentiment
of millions.   Such poems as " Excelsior" and
"A Psalm of Life" are world-poems and are
numbered among the "secular hymns " of
humanity.   That they are hackneyed is the
highest compliment that can be paid them ; it
means that they have entered into the world's
heart and are on every tongue.   Loftier praise
than this can sarcely be awarded any poet, for
it requires a rare adjustment of faculty to write
poems which have been so often parodied·but
are yet unspoiled, and, used in the common

utterance of two generations, are still as fresh as ever.

But the highest and most enduring fame of Longfellow must be based upon the calm and happy trust, the noble moral influence of his writings. Before his poetic career commenced he said in his prose poem, " Hyperion," that the surest blessedness was to do the thing that most wanted doing without a thought of fame, and he has assured us, in his poem on the despoiled ambitions of Belisarius, that

> " The plaudits of the crowd
> Are but the clatter of feet
> At midnight in the street,
> Hollow and restless and loud."

We can easily conceive that he has not worked for fame ; but if fame be ever worth the having, and if it can ever fill the heart with a genuine and pure delight, surely it must be the fame that is won by the exercise of rare gifts for the moral elevation and benefit of mankind. Such a fame is Longfellow's. He has set to all succeeding poets the noble example of great gifts employed for great uses, and has left behind him no soiled or evil page.

9

GEORGE ELIOT.

THE traveler who stands at the very foot
of a mountain is never conscious of its
vastness. It is only as he leaves it behind
him that its true proportions reveal themselves. Then, as he journeys far and farther
from its base, for the first time he realizes the
grandeur and sublimity of those summits which
were concealed from him when he stood beneath the very shadow of their walls. With
every step he takes, bigger and bluer swims up
into the sky the mountain's crest, changing
with the shifting light and growing distance,
frowning under the shadow of the thunder-
cloud, or softened in the evening stillness. It
is even so that the great presences of humanity impress their personality upon the ages.
They are rarely measured rightly by their immediate contemporaries, and one might add
by their earliest biographers. Boswells are
few, and the Boswell instinct is almost unique.
Forster can only give us a Forsterized Dickens,
and suggest ingenious doubts as to whether

he or Dickens really wrote *Dombey* and *David Copperfield*. Froude certainly gives us Carlyle, " warts and all ; " but the picture lacks balance and proportion, and the warts are seen through the magnifying-glass of an ultra-honesty which very much resembles malice. Mr. Cross gives us a bundle of letters and leaves George Eliot still a shadow and a name. It is charitable to assume that he has lived beneath her influence too completely to realize her greatness, and perhaps the same assumption may be true of the entire age in which her life was lived. We have not yet left the mountain far enough behind to realize its grandeur. But if we do not realize the grandeur we at least admit it ; and how great was the place George Eliot filled in modern literature we may measure by the impossibility of naming her successor.

The outline of George Eliot's early life is tolerably familiar to the public, and very great interest attaches to it. Her father was a remarkable man, of great natural shrewdness, individuality, and force of character. He was the son of a village carpenter, and many traits of his character are embodied in Adam Bede and Caleb Garth. His indomitable will, not

less than his business talents, raised him to the
position of land agent to Sir Roger Newdigate,
and throughout the part of Warwickshire where
he resided he was reverenced as a man of sterling and invincible uprightness.   Adam Bede
hated to see men drop their work the moment
the clock sounded, as though they grudged an
extra moment in their master's service; and
the same proud and generous spirit animated
Robert Evans.   He was incapable of mean-
ness and inflexible in duty.   Yet in the granite
of that strong nature, as is common in men
noted for their usual sternness, many a gentle
rill of tenderness welled up.   He was forty-six
when Marian was born, and "the little wench"
was very precious to her father.   Her mother
is said to have had a touch of Mrs. Poyser in
her—a woman of fine administrative ability in
the household, with a faculty of incisive speech
naturally running into epigram and wit, and
not seldom, probably, lacerating softer natures
with its sharp criticisms.   And there were un-
cles and aunts of the Glegg and Pullet type,
who no doubt thought the dreamy child a
very "strange little gell," and made her fly
with all the keener love to the refuge of the

strong father's affection. A very charming picture is given us of Mr. Robert Evans driving round the country-side with "the little gell" between his knees, the said little gell silently absorbing many a glimpse of landscape, or old gabled farm-house, and many a turn of humorous speech, which were all to swim up to the surface again in after years and be woven into the texture of her books. The most painful episode of the book is that which relates to the division which occurred in after-life between father and daughter on the subject of their theological views, the widowed father making up his mind to live alone rather than with a daughter who refused to go to church, and she for a time preferring the prospect of school-drudgery to submission. But the threatened separation never happened. The picture that glows before us in these early pages is of quiet home at Griff, a charming red brick, ivy-covered house on the Arbury estate—"the warm little nest where her affections were fledged." There George Eliot spent the first twenty-one years of her life.

An excellent passage in Mr. Cross's introduction puts before us vividly enough the

condition of the times in 1819, when Marian
Evans was born, and reminds us how far we
have moved :

"That Greater Britain (Canada and Australia) which to-day forms so large a reading
public was then scarcely more than a geo-
graphical expression, with less than half a
million of inhabitants, all told, where at present
there are eight millions; and in the United
States—where more copies of George Eliot's
works are now sold than in any other quarter
of the world—the population then numbered
less than ten millions, where to-day it is fifty-
five millions. Including Great Britain, these
English-speaking races have increased from
thirty millions in 1820 to one hundred millions
in 1884; and with the corresponding increase
in education we can form some conception how
a popular English writer's fame has widened
its circle."

As Mr. Cross justly observes, much of the
quality of George Eliot's writing is due to the
character of the times in which her youth was
lived. In 1819 the wheels of life ran slowly
along ruts of sweet, old-fashioned leisure, and
had not begun to break into flame with the

speed of modern energy. There was leisure to grow wise and shelter to grow ripe. The imagination had time to absorb its materials, and a large nature had space and peace in which to develop its powers. "Her roots were down in the pre-railroad, pre-telegraphic period, and her genius was the outcome of these conditions. Perhaps that is saying too much, but it certainly indicates an important truth. If solitude is necessary to the ease and tranquil strength, occasionally rising into majesty, and never destitute of force, which are the distinguishing qualities of George Eliot's style, it is easy to imagine how well such a style could grow in the remote serenity of a country house half a century ago, and how much more difficult it would be for any such style to take root and thrive amid the conditions of to-day life.

Nothing which George Eliot has written is so full of profound interest as the record of her own early life. That life has, indeed, been more than indicated in her own Maggie Tulliver. When she drew the picture of Maggie, with her pride and her affection, the one leading her into perpetual revolt, the other bring-

ing her back again humble and penitent, sub-
dued by the imperious need of being loved;
when she painted the gradual wakening of the
spiritual nature in Maggie, the desire for self-
sacrifice in perpetual conflict with the needs
and yearnings of a sensuous nature, the reverence for duty, the clear perception that
whatever failed that must be clung to, as with
a death-grip—in all this we have much of her
own spiritual portraiture. The young girl
who stands in the window of the old mill, absorbed in her first glimpse of Thomas à Kempis, thrilled with a strange awe, as if "wakened
in the night with a strain of solemn music,"
while the songs of that far-off voice echo for
the first time through her soul, saying, "Forsake thyself, resign thyself, and thou shalt enjoy much inward peace; then shall all vain
imaginations, evil perturbations, and superflu-
ous cares fly away; then shall immoderate
fear leave thee, and inordinate love shall die"
—this is Marian Evans at eighteen in the red
brick house at Griff. She, too, heard that
low penetrating music which has pierced and
soothed so many wayward hearts through the
long centuries, and drank it in as a draught of

life from the wells of God. Like Maggie, she read on and on in the old book, devouring eagerly the dialogues of the invisible Teacher, the pattern of sorrow, the source of all strength —with all the hurry of an imagination that could never rest in the present; and in the ardor of first discovery renunciation seemed to her the entrance into that satisfaction which she had so long been craving for in vain.

George Eliot never wrote a passage pervaded by more tender feeling than this passage describing how Maggie Tulliver, amid the miseries of her young life, first saw that heavenly vision of peace won out of sorrow and secret joy, kindled in spite of outward conditions of distress. As we read these early letters we can understand the spiritual emotion, the pathos and power, of this passage; it was drawn straight from the deeps of the writer's own most sacred experience. In that moment of spiritual revelation to George Eliot, as to many another, the secret of life seemed solved. She was swept by a strong tide, stronger than she knew, far away from her former conceptions of life, and in the delicious sense of surrender and renunciation never paused to ask whether she had not surrendered too much, whether such a tide might not ebb, whether such self-sacrifice as Thomas à Kempis taught might not be in fact self-effacement, and produce at last as strong a recoil in the repressed individuality.

In those days Marian Evans highly enjoyed Hannah More's letters, and found the "contemplation of so blessed a character as hers very salutary." She who in after years was to write that bitterly brilliant essay on "Other Worldliness," in which the works of Young are so mercilessly satirized, at eighteen is in love with his genius and strongly commends certain passages of his writings to her friends. There is a touch of asceticism in her thought which leads her to look upon marriage as an institution tending to dull the heavenly flame; and she "can only sigh for those who are multiplying earthly ties which, though powerful enough to detach their hearts and thoughts from heaven, are so brittle as to be liable to be snapped asunder at every breeze." Almost every-where in these early letters such sentences as these may be culled: "O, that we could live for eternity! that we could realize

its nearness! May the Lord give me such an
insight into what is truly good that I may not
rest content with making Christianity a mere
addendum to my pursuits, or with tacking it as
a fringe on my garments! May I seek to be
sanctified wholly!" To her aunt, Mrs. Samuel Evans—out of whose spiritual experience
and work as a Wesleyan preacher she fashioned
her Dinah Morris—she deplores her "lack of
humility and Christian simplicity, which makes
me willing to obtain credit for greater knowledge and deeper feeling than I really possess."

Novels she has little taste for, and considers
hurtful, and says: " Religious novels are more
hateful to me than merely worldly ones; they
are a sort of centaur or mermaid, and, like
other monsters that we do not know how
to class, should be destroyed for the public
good as soon as born. The weapons of the
Christian warfare were never sharpened at the
forge of romance." She complains that the
Oxford Tracts contain "a very confused and
unscriptural statement of the great doctrine
of justification," and " a disposition to frater-
nize with the mystery of iniquity." Her first
production ever clothed with the glory of

print is a poem on the death of St. Peter, which appeared in the *Christian Observer* for January, 1840, with an editorial note explaining that " M. A. E." is quite wrong in supposing that the Bible will be read in heaven. And in a letter written in her eighteenth year we have the germ of that tendency which in after-life led her to choose as her heroes and heroines common people, living homely lives and contending with the sordid troubles of an insignificant existence, and which led her to lay such eloquent stress upon the tragedy and passion which dwell in what we are pleased to call " common life." " I verily believe," she writes to Miss Lewis, " that in most cases it requires more of a martyr's spirit to endure with patience and cheerfulness daily crossings and interruptions of our petty desires and pursuits, and to rejoice in them, if they can be made to conduce to God's glory and our own sanctification, than even to lay down our lives for the truth." This is not merely a beautiful truth expressed with all the force and finish of George Eliot's maturest style, but is indicative of the tone of mind with which she habitually regarded human life, and which made farm

kitchens and carpenters' shops sufficient the-
aters for the noblest creations of her genius to
act out their simple heroisms or bitter trage-
dies.

In 1841 that acquaintance with the Brays
of Coventry commenced which had such an
important effect on George Eliot's subsequent
life. Mr. Bray had married a Miss Hennell,
and her brother Charles had published a book
entitled *An Inquiry into the Origin of Christianity*, which, in some important respects, an-
ticipated the rationalistic criticism and method
of Strauss. The perusal of this book had a
great effect on her mind, and completely altered
her views of the Christian religion. It directly
led to her subsequent translation of Strauss's
Leben Jesu, which was her first piece of real
literary work. But nothing is more remarkable in these letters and the record of her
entire life than the abundant evidence we
have that, whatever she ignored in Christian
truth, religious feeling never ceased to animate
her. While translating the work of Strauss
she had an ivory crucifix hung over her desk;
and to Miss Hennell she confesses " she is
Strauss-sick; it makes her ill, dissecting the

beautiful story of the crucifixion, and only the
sight of the Christ-image and picture make her
endure it." She writes thus of the journey to
Emmaus:

"That most beautiful passage in Luke's gospel! How universal is its significance! The
soul that has hopelessly followed its Jesus—its
impersonation of the highest and best—all in
despondency: its thoughts all refuted, its
dreams all dissipated! Then comes another
Jesus—another, but the same—the same highest best, only chastened—crucified instead of
triumphant; and the soul learns that this is
the true way to conquest and glory. And then
there is the burning of the heart, which assures
that this was the Lord—that this is the inspiration from above, the true Comforter that leads
into truth. But I am not a Methodist."

No, she was "not a Methodist;" but she had
drunk so deeply of the wells of early Methodist
theology that not even Strauss could prevent
this outburst of emotion, this tender, suppressed yearning of the lonely heart for some
more personal comforter than the "highest
best" of Positivism. It is a curious spectacle,
no doubt, the heart-sick translator of Strauss

only nerved to her work by the suspended crucifix, with its tokens of triumphant sorrow. We could more readily have understood the symbol of that divine anguish arresting the hand that was slowly reducing its reality to a fable. But we must remember that in George Eliot we have to do with a nature wonderfully complex and intricate; a masculine intellect allied to more than usually sensitive emotions ; a mind capable of the severest study, the subtlest strategies of thought, held in check by all the clinging tenderness of a nature capable of passionate attachments and perpetually yearning for some responding love on which it could repose—some object on which it might lavish the wealth of its affections.

It is absolutely necessary to bear this in mind if we are to hold any clew at all to the nature of George Eliot and the motives of her life. No one can read her letters without re-marking on the facility with which she took up new friendships and the almost girlish effusive-ness which characterizes her letters, even when she was in the last stage of life, to her recent as well as her old friends. That hunger for love which led Maggie Tulliver into so many errors

was precisely the master-passion in the heart
of her creator; but while in George Eliot's
case the crowning mistake which Maggie nobly
fought down was actually committed, yet, by
virtue of that very tenderness, neither Strauss,
nor Frederick Harrison, nor G. H. Lewes, nor
any other creature could wholly close the door
of her heart against the exiled Christ of the
intellect. The woman who pictured Dinah
Morris preaching on the village green and
praying with the penitent Hetty Sorrel in
prison; who, in the highest hour of her destiny, makes Maggie Tulliver, amid the fierce
stress of mortal anguish, turn from the golden
future to the hard, bleak waste of life-long
renunciation, crying, " There are memories and
affections and longings after a perfect goodness that have such a strong hold on me I
couldn't live at peace if I put the shadow of a
willful sin between myself and God;" who in
her greatest story makes the modern world
thrill again before the spiritual force and intensity of Savonarola, as once all Florence thrilled
and trembled when the thunder of his voice
pealed through the Duomo—this woman had
tasted the mysteries of a religious experience

foreign enough to the shallow amiability and self-complacency of such a nature as that of Mr. George Henry Lewes. She was "not a Methodist ; " but like many other persons who would disclaim the title both her life and her art owed more than she supposed to those religious influences which molded her in early days.

In any attempt to fix the place of George Eliot among English writers it will be necessary to lay stress upon this strange union in her of what are often opposites. Every page of her life gives evidence of the intensity of her emotions, the space and energy of her intellect, and the strength of her religious feeling. Much might be written upon the enormous capacity for work which she possessed, her splendid grasp of abstruse sciences, her use of scientific illustrations in her prose and poetry, the delicacy, subtlety, and acumen of her mind ; and these are the more remarkable not merely because they existed in a woman with more than ordinary susceptibility of nature and more than common tenderness of affection, but because they were found in a woman who had built up her culture in lonely isolation
10

from great centers of thought, and amid distressing physical conditions which made it often
true that her address was, "Grief Castle, on
the River of Gloom, in the Valley of Dolor."
The unique position George Eliot holds in
English literature is due to this combination
of gifts, and is at once indicated by comparison. Take the three greatest names in modern
fiction—Scott, Dickens, and Thackeray—and
compare with them and their works George
Eliot and hers. In Scott is broad health and
freedom, breadth of sky, clearness of atmosphere, not less in the outlook and character of
his own mind than in his presentation of artistic
effects; but nowhere does he show himself
penetrated by any sense of the mystery and
complexity of life. He writes with the good-
natured ease of a man blessed with an excellent
digestion and familiar with broad moors and
sweet country air; who, in his own life, has
never sounded the deeper notes of tragedy
and never known the bitter throes of anguish.
Dickens is always a boy in his humor, and
exaggerates his tragedy, as a man would who
relies for his materials on imagination rather
than experience; and, moreover, he seldom

gives us any sense of intellectual resource. Thackeray, perhaps, impresses us with the greatest sense of intellectual powers; and in his best and most serious writing is most penetrated by religious feeling. Each is great in his sphere, and a more or less interesting personality.

But George Eliot is much more. She is a great thinker and a great scholar who chooses to write tales, but who might as readily have written histories and philosophies. It is characteristic that she was thirty-seven before she attempted fiction, and then—in spite of Mr. Lewes's opinion that she lacked imagination and dramatic power—with such success as to place her instantly in the rank of great masters. Her popularity only deepened in her mind her sense of responsibility, a sense which latterly became a burden very heavy to be borne, for she never regarded herself in any other light than that of a teacher. She brought to the novelist's art wide scholarship, splendid intellect, and profound experience, and held it in trust as a ministry. One fails anywhere to discern personal vanity in her in relation to her own works; every-where one does discern this

intense sense of responsibility. The result is
that she is so much more than a novelist that
occasionally she is less than one; the burden
of her teaching is too great for the resources
of her romance, and it is the voice of the
prophet which is sometimes heard instead of
the cunning music of the story-teller. But
another consequence is that her fiction is
wrought with a majesty and power which give
it a category of its own and secure for it a
noble place in English literature. It is superb
fiction; but it is much more than fiction.

George Eliot seldom spoke of her own
works even to intimate friends, but in the last
year of her life she once asked Mr. Cross a
question concerning their general effect upon
his mind, which led him to reply that he felt
the general effect to be profoundly sad. She
was grieved and disappointed with the answer.
In spite of endless physical depressions she
herself possessed an indomitable cheerfulness,
and she naturally supposed she had communi-
cated some portion of that cheerfulness to her
writings. Yet unquestionably Mr. Cross was
right. The dominant chord, sometimes almost
lulled into a distant murmur but never silent,

and continually swelling up into tragic passion
and pain, is sadness. Her humor passes like a
ripple of swift sunshine or laughter, but the old
gray sky closes up again and the smothered wail
of pain makes itself heard. The central point of
her philosophy is that there is a continuity in
actions which cannot be broken, and that nothing but an inflexible regard for duty and a
perpetual willingness to sacrifice our own happiness to supreme moral purposes, or the
happiness of others, can save the individual
life from shipwreck or mutilation. She never
shows us good springing out of evil; mere
optimistic folk may teach that comforting doctrine; but she walks in the light of common
day and in the presence of the unvarnished
realities of life, and prefers to enforce the more
terrible truth that evil springs out of evil, and
can produce nothing but evil. There are no
arresting angels in the path ; healing and comforting angels there may be, but the bitter
consequences of wrong-doing must be paid to
the uttermost farthing notwithstanding. With
an almost cruel insistency, or an insistency
which would be cruel but for the sympathy
and pity of the writer, she follows the clew of

the first evil step in its unwinding, and forces
us to admit the inevitable recompense, the irreparable pain.   Every book she has written is
charged with this stern truth, and its plot ultimately reaches this *dénouement*.   Hetty Sorrel's vanity and shallowness, her disregard for
those homely traditions which have their roots
in the dim past and make a code of duty for
homely people, with all the hard selfishness
which lay under that pretty childishness, work
out inevitably the tragedy of her life, and are
in fact the very elements out of which that
tragedy springs.   Godfrey Cass's first error, in
concealing what he ought to have confessed,
brings a whole string of errors with it, stretch-
ing over a life-time, until, after twenty years,
the bitter revelation has to be made, and the
cry is wrung from him : " There's debts we
can't pay like money debts, by paying extra
for the years that have slipped by.   Marner
was right in what he said about a man turning
away a blessing from his door; it falls to somebody else.   I wanted to pass for childless once ;
I shall pass for childless now against my wish."

But it is in Romola and in the character of
Tito Melema that this lesson is driven home

with the most merciless force. The smooth
young Greek, with his beautiful face and happy
smile—who could think of him as Judas?
Yet perchance Judas

> " Had eyes of starry blue,
> And lips like thine, that gave the traitor-kiss."

It is one of the minor lessons George Eliot is
fond of teaching, that faces can be masks as
well as mirrors; it is the heart and not the
face that makes the traitor. Tito shrinks from
inflicting pain as from suffering it; he wishes
to be happy himself, and has the most benevo-
lent desires for the happiness of the whole human race. But he is thoroughly resolved to
be happy at all costs; and while he deplores
the necessity of making the anguish of others
part of that cost, yet he accepts the necessity.
It is unpleasant; he would much rather have
gained his base Paradise without injury to any
body; but he is quietly resolved not to forego
it on that account. From the moment he refuses his first obvious duty of rescuing the old
scholar who had lived for him the wrong step
is taken which leads onward through an increasing maze of difficulties. As a direct consequence of his first prevarication he finds

himself under the unpleasant necessity of de-
nouncing his foster-father as a madman, of
sending him in chains to prison, and, by another series of events springing from the first,
of becoming a traitor to his wife and the be-
trayer of his party.   There is no more profoundly subtle portrait in English literature
than Tito's; and its artistic truth is as absolute
as the technical skill with which it is perfected.
Its moral power is even more wonderful.   To
the last Tito has never succeeded in becoming
a hardened and thorough-paced villain; the
ill he does is repugnant to him, and he would
much rather not have done it.   But his only
guide is desire, and his only principle of action
present ease and pleasure.   And he forgets, or
has never recognized, that grim, indefeasible
truth which George Eliot makes the soul of
her teaching in this as in so many books:
"Our deeds are like children that are born to
us; they live and act apart from our will.
Nay, children may be strangled, but deeds
never; they have an indestructible life both in
and out of our consciousness."

For this moral teaching the world owes a
great debt of gratitude to George Eliot.   But

it was inevitable that a series of books all
more or less permeated with such teaching, all
striking this deep chord of the irreparable, all
omitting, or else including but faint, far-off
snatches of that sweeter music of a divine
hope, a divine restoration, should be profoundly sad. Even the humor of George
Eliot is tinged with this sadness; it is bitter-
sweet, and is akin to pity. It springs from the
active contact of a high and broad mind with
narrow and confined intelligences, reading their
dim thoughts by a wider light and measuring
their homely ways by a larger standard. If
Dickens had painted the Gleggs and the Pul-
lets we should have felt that he himself enjoyed the fun he made, and we should have
caught our contagion of laughter straight from
his own lips. But George Eliot's humor is a
boomerang; it makes the circle of laughter
and ends in pity. We feel that she is not
really laughing herself at all. She is thinking
how sad a sight it is to look upon people im-
prisoned in such small traditions and unable to
perceive the larger life that throbs around
them; and while she cannot help describing
the "ways of the Dodson family" with evi-

dent relish she is full of gentle pity and regret.
She herself was, probably, quite unconscious
that this understrain of deep feeling made itself felt through her humor, and hence her
disappointment when more than one intimate
friend confessed to the realization of this sense
of general sadness produced by her works.
But it is an unquestioned element, and it may,
perhaps, be said that no writer who has done
so much to move our laughter has written so
much to make us sad.

And though it is not a pleasant thing to say,
yet it must be confessed that we rise from the
perusal of this life with the consciousness that
the somberness was in the life itself, and in the
result of a wrong step which casts its shadow to
the end. At the most crucial point of her own
career George Eliot did what the whole bulk
of her teaching condemns with such majestic
sternness: she forgot the inexorable regard for
duty, the imperious necessity of purchasing no
personal joy by the grief of others or her own
errors; the clear need of sacrificing personal
joy to the wise traditions of universal law and
order which that teaching every-where enforces
as the first condition of a truly noble life.

It has been said that from that wrong step sprang the real development of her life, and that by it was wrought the new intellectual force which gave the world her novels. But there is no evidence of this, and we think George Eliot herself would have been the first to resent such an inference with scorn. She would have said that better no such books were written than written at the price of wrong, and we can readily imagine with what force and eloquence of noble sentiment she would have treated such a position had it found a place in her fiction. As it was she did say, through the lips of Maggie Tulliver, "Many things are difficult and dark to me; but I can see one thing quite clearly, that I must not, cannot seek my own happiness by sacrificing others. Love is natural; but surely pity and faithfulness and memory are natural too. And they would live in me still, and punish me if I did not obey them. I should be haunted by the suffering I had caused. Faithfulness and constancy mean something else besides doing what is easiest and pleasantest to ourselves. They mean renouncing whatever is opposed to the reliance others have in

us—whatever would cause misery to those
whom the course of our lives has made depend-
ent on us." Is it too much to suppose that
here it is George Eliot herself who speaks—
that in spite of all intellectual sophistries with
which she might impose upon the moral sense,
that sensitive and noble nature, that delicate
and shrinking womanliness felt the sting, and
was indeed haunted by the suffering one wrong
step had caused? It is true there is no evidence of any remorse in her published letters,
but there is abundant evidence in her stories.
The constant reiteration of one painful theme
is proof of how large a place it filled in her
own experience. Whenever she approaches it
her tone deepens into solemnity, and her message is delivered with intense, even anguished
moral earnestness. No writer of fiction has
treated the temptations of passion with a nobler moral force or insight, and none has dwelt
upon them more persistently. But this very
fact is in itself an indication of that concealed suffering which confesses itself by sympathy with the suffering of others, and it is
impossible to dissociate the sadness of George
Eliot's books from the error of her life.

The whole life of George Eliot was pervaded by her intellectual energy and devoted to incessant intellectual toil. She said she began "Romola" a young woman, and it left her an old one. She spared no effort to make her work complete; and her sense of responsibility to the public, after their first recognition of her great powers, led her to cultivate those powers to the utmost for the public service. The very completeness of that culture reacted disastrously upon her later novels; but just as it has been said no other poet but Milton could have moved under the immense weight of classical learning contained in the "Paradise Lost," so it may be asserted any other novelist than George Eliot would have been stifled under the trappings of so encyclopedic a culture as hers. Her physical sufferings were not less than Carlyle's, but her views of life were never jaundiced by them, nor her tongue envenomed. There is a dignity about her last days which reminds us of the last days of Milton. Like Milton, she always began her day with some chapters from the Bible, and particularly delighted in reading aloud the finer passages of Isaiah, Jeremiah, and St. Paul. Her voice had

"organ-like tones" in it, and when she read
the Bible, and the elder English poets, its deep
sadness added greatly to the solemnity and
majesty of the rhythm. In Shakespeare and
Milton, and latterly in Wordsworth, she found
constant companionship; and four lines from
the "Samson Agonistes" she was accustomed
to repeat with a fullness of effect not to be forgotten:

> "But what more oft, in nations grown corrupt,
> And by their vices brought to servitude,
> Than to love bondage more than liberty,
> Bondage with ease than strenuous liberty?"

She keenly watched the social life of her time,
and with all its intellectual movements she was
intimately acquainted. In her the thirst for
knowledge was never slaked, and the ardor of
the intellect never dimmed. To the last no
shadow fell across that spacious mind; no faculty lost its edge, no function of thought gave
intimation of decay. There was no darkening
of the stage before the curtain fell—it fell
silently and swiftly upon a brilliant intellect at
the very culmination of its powers. At her
death there was found within reach of the
lifeless hand one pathetic memorial of the

past, which neither change of creed nor state could exile; it had accompanied her through all the strange ways which lay between the obscure girl-life at Griff and the famous years of mature womanhood in London—it was a well-worn copy of Thomas à Kempis.

GEORGE MEREDITH:

HIS METHOD AND HIS TEACHING.

I READ the other day, in an article which professed to be critical, the somewhat remarkable statement that there were at least fifty novelists who could have written *Oliver Twist* better than Dickens wrote it. I was sincerely glad to hear it, for I had no notion that English fiction was so liberally endowed in these latter days, and I wish I could believe it. As a matter of fact, unfortunately, every one who knows any thing will know that this statement is ludicrously false, and he will know how it came to be made. It is the result of the new method of criticism, which writes its "appreciations" or "depreciations" at random, and bases its judgments entirely on the comparison of things between which there is no likeness, and therefore ought to be no comparison. Criticism without comparison is impossible, but under such a system it becomes necessary to depreciate one author in order to "appreciate" another, and the main result is wholesale confusion of thought and utter blindness of judgment.

Now, Mr. Meredith is at the present moment in great peril from this species of writing. There is a Meredith-cult in progress, and every one who loves literature will rejoice that this is so in so far as it means that after thirty years of scandalous neglect the public has at last discovered that there is a writer of first-rate genius in its midst. But is it really necessary to sneer at Dickens and disparage Thackeray and George Eliot in order to convince us of the excellence of George Meredith? Why make comparisons which bring no light, but rather make confusion worse confounded, which not only do not help us toward a true interpretation of Meredith, but destroy the very means by which any true interpretation becomes possible? It is perfectly true that Dickens could not have written the *Ordeal of Richard Feverel*, but it is equally true that Meredith could not have written *Oliver Twist*; and again it is true that each is a work of genius. The fifty gentlemen who could have written *Oliver Twist* are of strangely retiring

11

and modest disposition, for up to the present
moment we have had no sign of the presence
of any one of them.   When any one of them
has written a half-dozen pages as deeply tragic
as the murder of Nancy and the death of Bill
Sikes we shall hear of him without fail ; and
if we have not heard of him it is surely because he has not yet accomplished that remarkable feat.   No ; we shall not arrive at the
truth about any body by simply disparaging
his neighbors.   George Meredith must be taken
upon his own merits, and in no possible case
that might be suggested is the comparative
method of criticism more futile.   He stands
by himself, a strong and lonely figure, on a
coign of vantage all his own, uncompanied and
unclassed, impressive by his very loneliness not
less than by his strength, a man supremely indifferent to the world and its cackle of praise
or disparagement, who from the first has
waited for the world to come up to him, and
has never sought to descend to the world.
He has the majestic isolation of the mountain
peak that does not appear to belong to any
range, a Matterhorn, sharply divided from its
fellows, serrated and solitary, rejoicing in its

own splendors of dawn and sunset, starry eminence and glory, while other peaks share a
common day and night. If such a man is to
be understood it can only be by patient study of
his style and teaching, and this can only be
undertaken and accomplished by free minds—
by minds that are open to receive new impres-
sions without prejudice and to register them
without reference to older standards.

Having said so much it is natural to ask,
How is it that it has taken so long for George
Meredith to become known? Matterhorns
cannot very well be hid. Why have so few
persons noticed such a presence in so long a
period as thirty years? If we take the date
of his first book, the Poems of 1851, the period
is really forty years; but it is sufficient for our
purpose to take the date of his first great novel,
Richard Feverel, which appeared in 1859. Since
that date he has published nine complete novels,
besides various short tales and poems. How is
it that they have made comparatively so little
impression on the public mind? To revert to
my image for a moment, I may reply that
it by no means follows that because there
is a Matterhorn every one will know it. Great

peaks, like all other great things, after all, have
to be discovered, and for centuries travelers
may pass the mouth of some valley which
holds a Matterhorn without any impulse to
penetrate its solitude or any notion that it is
the pathway to a splendor. It counts for
little, as a detraction from genius, that men
have had to wait long for recognition. In our
own generation Wordsworth and Browning
wrote for thirty years without earning enough
money to buy them porridge, and Carlyle
was on the very brink of ruin before the
tide turned. But perhaps these names in
themselves are sufficient to explain the phe-
nomenon. Each brought something new for
which the world was unprepared, a new teaching and a new style. When this happens the
only consolation of the author is to reflect that
his writing

> " Is not meat
> For little people and for fools,"

and to await with patience the hour when those
who are wiser, the true " aristocracy," will recognize the truth, and force its recognition
upon the dull mind of the world.

The delay of recognition with George Mer-

edith is due first to the novelty of his style.
It is brilliant beyond example, but at times obscure in almost equal degree.   It is, however,
far oftener brilliant than obscure.   To those
who love splendor, subtlety, and felicity of
diction, combined with the most penetrating
and suggestive thought, the writing of George
Meredith is an unboundaried paradise.   Roam
where you will, a profusion of things dear to
the delicate and discerning palate are found.
Or, to change the figure, never was there so
coruscating a style.   The page perpetually
breaks in star-sparkles ; it flashes with all sorts
of pyrotechnic displays, it is volcanic with
eruptive radiance.   Sometimes it is almost mis-
chievously coruscating, as though a boy ex-
ploded crackers under you for the mere pleasure of seeing you jump.   But one never knows
how soon or suddenly the fire may go out, and
you may find yourself plunged into the darkest
by-ways of obscurity.   Mr. Meredith has described Carlyle's style, and in doing so has par-
tially described his own :

" A style resembling either early architect-
ure or utter dilapidation, so loose and rough it
seemed ; a wind-in-the-orchard style, that tum-

bled down here and there an appreciable fruit
with uncouth bluster; sentences without com-
mencements running to abrupt endings and
smoke, like waves against a sea-wall, learned
dictionaries giving a hand to street-slang, and
accents falling on them haphazard, like slant
rays from driving clouds; all the pages in a
breeze, the whole book producing a sort of
electrical agitation in the mind and joints."

Neither of Carlyle nor Meredith is this description wholly true; but, as Carlyle might
have said, "it is significant of much" in both.
To complain of too great brilliance is, no doubt,
a novel complaint, yet in Mr. Meredith's case
it is a very real one. Conceive a concert
wherein all the music is *allegro*, or a gallery
entirely full of Turner's most gorgeous sunsets,
and you have a not inapt illustration of the
effect produced by a continuous reading of
George Meredith. The most brilliant thing
suffers by a want of contrast. The last marvelous movement in a great sonata is all the
more striking by contrast with that which has
preceded it; the finest Turner is yet finer if
we see it after having seen some study of soft
and tender grays. We miss the point of rest

almost altogether in Mr. Meredith's work. He
is so infinitely vivacious, versatile, and witty,
so fertile in jest and epigram, so agile in the
leaps and glances of his thought, so wayward
and surprising, so conspicuously acute and
clever, that less nimble minds pant breathless
behind him, and even the nimblest have a difficulty in keeping pace with him. " She ran
ahead of his thoughts like nimble fire," he
says in one place of Mrs. Caroline Grandison.
It is a just description of his own treatment
of his readers ; and sometimes the fire we have
followed with panting eagerness suddenly
dances a will-o'-the-wisp fantasy of mirth and
leaves us knee-deep in the bog. When once
we become used to his method no writer can
afford so much intellectual exhilaration ; but it
is little wonder, when we consider it, that the
regular novel-reader is bewildered by so uncommon a guide and prefers some one much
duller and safer. Intellectual gymnastics, however brilliant, are not what that patient and
somewhat dull creature, " the general reader,"
looks for in a novel.

It is altogether too late to enter upon the
question so often raised in connection with

Mr. Meredith's work, whether science ought
to find place in novels ; the question is rather
how large a space ought science to occupy.
If this is a scientific age, and if the novel holds
the mirror up to the age, science must needs
be adequately reflected in it.   Moreover, as
one of Mr. Meredith's critics has truly said,
the way of advance in English fiction lies
through George Eliot and George Meredith—
that is, through the only two novelists of our
time who have come to their task with a complete scientific equipment.   Is their work the
better or worse for this equipment ?   It may
be answered that it is both.   After all, the
novel is not a psychological, and still less a
physiological, treatise, and there are moments
in the writing of both George Eliot and
George Meredith when it becomes this and
nothing more. The more a novelist knows the
better will he write ; but when he pauses in his
story to display his knowledge he becomes a
pedant and ceases to be a novelist. The worst
fault of Browning also lies in this ; there are
times when his poetry runs into pedantry, and
the reader of the "Paradise Lost" will note the
same tendency in Milton.   But it is possible,

and it is common, to exaggerate these blemishes, and people who do not care to be at any
trouble in their reading triumphantly push
these blemishes forward as an excuse for their
intellectual indolence. To such people, I suppose, poetry and fiction are simply ingenious
relaxations for the idle moments of life, of
which they have too many, and they naturally
demand the old commonplaces of pursuing
love and ultimate marriage-bells as the beginning and end of fiction, and resent a style of
fiction which is charged with the gravest matter and is meant to make men think. Toward
such readers George Meredith, and not less
George Eliot and Browning, take up an attitude of irreconcilable defiance. They do so
because they regard their art as a serious business. They are of Milton's temper, and approach their task with a solemn invocation
that what is dark in them may be illumined,
what is weak strengthened, that they may rise
to the height of their great argument. A
sacred fire burns in them, for they are prophets,
not hirelings; voices, not echoes; artists, not
artificers. Milton, George Eliot, and Browning have already triumphed and compelled the

world to listen ; will not George Meredith also triumph in due season ?

I have stated the defects of George Meredith, but I am bound to add that they are the defects of great qualities, and that they have been greatly exaggerated by people incapable of recognizing the qualities. If I am sometimes wearied with the constant dazzle of the style, on the whole I am only too glad to find a style that is capable of dazzling, and I may add that I am seldom wearied. If I mention its occasional obscurity, I emphasize the fact that the obscurity is only occasional, and that as a rule the style is absolutely lucid. Nothing can be more unjust than to say that George Meredith cannot tell a story or that his style is consistently obscure. The bulk of his stories are admirably conceived and executed, and for the most part the style is marvelous in its suppleness, its unflagging force and grace, its subtlety of flavor and suggestion, its flashes of inspiration, its intense concision, its actual splendor and poetry of phrase, its searching directness and nervous strength. He is a prose Browning, and his phrases are even more haunting than Browning's. He is the comrade and suc-

cessor of George Eliot, but is George Eliot's
master both in force of intellect and poetic
magnificence of diction.

Why, then, we ask again, has it taken thirty
years for Mr. Meredith to be known, and even
now not widely known? The real reason lies
in the fact that he was not the universal note
of the great popular writers.

Dickens, in his best work, and in spite of
much that was tawdry, had that note; and
George Eliot, also, in spite of much that was
stiff and scholastic, at least in her earlier
volumes. *David Copperfield* has a charm for
the least and most cultured, and so has *Adam
Bede*. The shopman and the student alike
read them, and each feels the charm, though it
may be through widely differing channels.
But great as are *The Ordeal of Richard Feverel*
and *The Egoist*, they are not conceived on that
broadly human scale which is bound to draw
all eyes, to move all hearts. They have height
rather than breadth, a quality that is Miltonic
rather than Shakespearean. They appeal irre-
sistibly to the cultured, but scarcely at all to
the crowd. Style, whether too brilliant or too
obscure, science, whether too obtrusively or

too frequently thrust to the front, would not
be sufficient barriers to dismay the mass of
readers if the story itself struck the universal
note and appealed to the deep heart of humanity.

To recur again to a name which is insepara-
ble from Meredith's, we may say that he and
Browning stand in the same category.   It is
impossible to suppose that either can be widely
read.   Browning is not a people's poet, nor is
Meredith a people's novelist.   But in spite of
this Browning, in his teaching and his influence,
stands at the back of all the most influential
teachers of our day, and is daily being re-in-
terpreted by a thousand lips to ten thousands
of persons who are ignorant of his poetry.   In
the same way Meredith is a fruitful force,
working not directly but indirectly on the
mass of readers, not in his own person so
much as in a far wider degree through the
persons of others who have received the impact
of his teaching.   It is perhaps not as we could
wish it, and not as he could wish it.   But if it
be for the present a thing inevitable there is
this compensation, that as the race progresses
he will become more and more visible in the

general life, and may be read together with Browning by new generations, when those who had their reward in this life are utterly forgotten.

The two great weapons in which Meredith excels are satire and humor. The satire is never less than excellent, for in the mere literary finish of his biting epigrams he is unsurpassed by any writer of English, either past or present. The fault of the satire is that it is not kindly, and it can be cruel. It is as keen as a surgeon's knife, and as cold. It lays bare all the hidden disease of the human soul, and cuts relentlessly, almost savagely, through the intervening filaments. Not in all literature is there to be found so terrible an exposition of selfishness as in the character of Sir Willoughby Patterne, the Egoist. If it were possible to light up a human body from the inside, so that it should become transparent to us, like a glass bee-hive, in which we see every movement of busy wing or tentacle, so that in like manner we might discern every little beating nerve of man, every throb and palpitation of remotest vein and artery, it would be an apt figure of how Meredith treats the soul of man. He

conceals nothing; he concedes nothing; he
simply flashes his terrible search-light into the
secret places of the heart, and things explain
themselves.   Coiling one inside the other, restless with vehement and loathsome vitality, we
see the mass of serpentine motives, the mean
and wicked impulses, which lurk in the bottom
of the human ego.   Pleasant?—no, it is not
pleasant; but how true it is! How wholesome
it is for us to be driven sometimes into this
searching analysis of ourselves! We pause a
hundred times in the reading of the *Egoist*
and shudder, for we have found out something
about ourselves which we did not suspect, or
of which we were fearfully and faintly conscious, as of a skeleton in the cupboard, known
to us, but judiciously and gratefully ignored.
Mr. Meredith refuses to be our accomplice in
any such deception.   He forces us to face the
ghastly secret of the human cupboard. "Sacred
reality," he tells us, is the goddess he worships;
and he argues that it cannot be wise or right for
any of us to go about in ignorance of what we
really are.   His satire is the child of relentless
truth; it is indeed truth itself, naked, severe,
uncompromising.   When we close the *Egoist*

we feel as if we have already stood before the
judgment-seat of God.

No more striking example of this rigid satir-
ical analysis is to be found than in Mr. Meredith's exposure of what Sir Willoughby's desire for purity in woman really means. He
demands of his betrothed that she should be
cloistral. "Women of mixed essences, shad-
ing off the divine to the considerably lower,
were outside his vision of women." He
demands "purity infinite, spotless bloom."
The commonplace observer will at once say,
Of how admirable and clean a nature must be
this man who can be content with nothing less
than "purity infinite" in woman. Not at all,
says Mr. Meredith; entirely the reverse. It is
nothing but a "voracious æsthetic gluttony."
"It has its foundation in the sensual," and this
vast and dainty exacting appetite is lineally
"the great-grandson of the Hoof." Why
does he frantically demand this immaculate,
this more than human bloom? It is the exac-
tion of a gluttonous, sensual appetite. It is
more than that; for him there must needs be
fashioned "a perfect specimen designed for
the elect of men." There the secret is out;

the demand is but another tentacle of that ink-spitting cuttlefish Egoism, which works uneasily in the mud of the human heart, and stretches itself on all sides in insatiable craving. "And," adds Mr. Meredith, "the capaciously strong in soul among women will ultimately detect an infinite grossness in the demand for purity infinite, spotless bloom." What you have supposed the demand of austerity is the passionate shriek of voluptuousness, and the strong-souled among women will find you out.

Mr. Meredith's satire allied to analysis is sometimes cruel, but when it is allied to humor it is delightful. It is then the smack of the sea-salt that gives edge to the sunny breeze. He can be droll, quaint, genial; he can jest and gambol like a boy or shout with Homeric laughter. He who has not read *Evan Harrington* has before him several hours of unmitigated laughter. For broad humor—in one or two instances a trifle too broad for good taste—it would be hard to surpass that memorable cricket supper at the Green Dragon, Fallowfield, and the eccentric behavior of John Raikes thereat. The hat of John Raikes

alone is provocative of infinite mirth. "I
mourn my hat. He is old—I mourn him yet
living. The presence of crape on him signi-
fies he shall ne'er have a gloss again. The
fact is my hat is a burden in the staring crowd.
A hat like this should counsel solitude." In
another spirit, but as genially humorous, is the
famous description of Mrs. Caroline Grandison,
in *Richard Feverel.* "She was a colorless lady,
of an unequivocal character, living upon drugs,
and governing her husband and the world from
her sofa. Woolly Negroes blessed her name
and whiskered John Thomases deplored her
weight." She had rapidly produced eight
daughters, and felt the solemnity of woman's
mission. A son was denied her. Her husband, the quite unobjectionable gentleman,
lost heart after the arrival of the eighth, and
surrendered his mind to more frivolous pursuits. After that disappointing eighth she also
lost heart and "relapsed upon religion and
little dogs." But to give samples of Mr.
Meredith's humor were an endless task. It
runs through a hundred variations, from the
keenest to the broadest; it smacks of Jingle
and of Falstaff; it is sometimes roaring farce,

12

at others finished comedy; it is acute, genial,
caustic; it is now hilarious with boyish buoyancy and good spirits, now the product of masculine good sense and piercing insight, now a
shaft of laughter playing round a fountain of
tears; and, widely as it differs, running through
the gamut from the verbal quip to the profoundly human delineation, from merely comic
to half-tragic laughter, it is a pervasive element, with which all his books are lavishly endowed. As a mere humorist Meredith is as
superior to those ephemeral writers who pass
as such to-day as is Shakespeare to Douglas
Jerrold.

To Meredith, as to Thackeray, and with
equal ignorance and lack of insight, the term
cynic has been generally applied. If the
cynic is he who sneers at good, then no man
has less deserved the reproach. But when
such terms are used no one stops to consider
what they imply, and to call a man a cynic is
the only refuge of Philistine mediocrity, which
above all things dreads satire, and is afraid of
being laughed at for not understanding what
breeds laughter in others. I am willing to admit that there is sometimes a disagreeable flavor

in some of Meredith's scenes and phrases. One knows not how to define it, except to say that in such cases his robust masculinity touches in a fugitive fashion the verge of grossness. But of cynicism, of the spirit which mocks and derides, he has no trace; on the contrary, one is struck by the broad humanity of his writings, their essential buoyancy and good humor. And this is the more remarkable when we recollect that he has been condemned by the public to thirty years of almost total neglect, during which period he has had the mortification of seeing a score of writers with not a tithe of his genius press to the front and become the acknowledged representatives of English fiction. The *Ordeal* of George Meredith will make one of the most surprising chapters of that history of literature which our sons will write one day. For him, as for Browning, has been ordained a quarter of a century of deaf ears and mocking mouths; and how much does it say for the genuine greatness of each that they were able to keep a tranquil soul, an unembittered mind, and emerge from the cloud of neglect as the great optimists of their generation!

If we will take the trouble to analyze this so-called cynicism we shall see at once that its component elements are really moral intensity and love of "sacred reality." To tell the plain truth is often to say a bitter thing, and for a good many people any thing bitter is called cynical. And the supreme moral value of George Meredith's writing is its absolute witness to truth. He glosses over nothing. He sees clearly "the reddened sources" from which even the noblest passions spring. He is profoundly convinced that we can gain nothing in the long run by ignoring any element of truth about ourselves. To leave the body out of consideration in our epitome of man is as fatal a blunder as to ignore the soul. To collect only the finest qualities of a man or woman into a sort of odorous nosegay and call that human nature is to commit an outrage on justice. The earth grows weeds as well as flowers, and so does human nature. Let us have then the whole truth, and nothing but the truth; it will do us less harm to know every thing than to know only what it will please us best to know. That is the great lesson of his greatest book, *Richard Feverel*; and

never was a lesson taught with more impressive power.   The system, as he derisively calls
it, that marvelous system which is to produce
a perfect youth by picking and choosing among
the elements of things, by building walls here
to close up dangerous paradises, and opening
gate-ways there into sterile moral Saharas, by
twisting this proclivity into grotesqueness, like
a bruised vine upon a pole, and diverting the
natural course of that taste or passion till it
makes for itself feculent puddles instead of
flowing purely in its natural bed—this system,
carefully pieced together, mechanical, rigid,
meant to mutilate life at every point, and produce perfection by mutilation, in the end works
nothing but havoc, ruin, and death to all whom
it concerns.   And the secret of its failure lies
in the fact that it is not based upon the truth
of things.   "Great is truth, and must prevail,"
is the constant chant of George Meredith;
and not less passionately than Carlyle does he
perpetually affirm that truth is always wholesome, and a half-truth is the worst of lies.

The moral intensity of Meredith often becomes almost prophetic in its passion.   "You
cannot cheat nature," he insists over and over

again. Nowhere in fiction is there a more
tremendous sermon on the inevitable consequences of sin than in that chapter of *Richard
Feverel* called "The Wild Oats Plea."   Every
youth should read it; it is a prophet's scroll
to be thrust into his hand as he steps over the
threshold of boyhood into the fullness of manhood. Sir Austin Feverel calls upon two ancient intimates, Lord Heddon and Darley
Absworthy, "useful men though gouty, who
had sown in their time a fine crop of wild oats,
and advocated the advantage of doing so, seeing that they did not fancy themselves the
worse for it."   He found one with an imbecile
son and the other with consumptive daughters.
"So much," he wrote in his note-book, "for
the wild oats theory!"

Darley was proud of his daughters' white
and pink skins. Beautiful complexions, he
called them. The eldest was in the market,
immensely admired. There was something
poetic about her. She intimated that she was
robust, but toward the close of their conversa-
tion her hand would now and then travel to
her side, and she breathed painfully an instant,
saying, "Isn't it odd? Dora, Adela, and my-

self, we all feel the same queer sensation—
about the heart; I think it is—after talking
much."

Sir Austin nodded and blinked sadly, ex-
claiming to his soul, "Wild oats! wild oats!"

Lord Heddon vehemently preached wild
oats also. He was of opinion that a lad is all
the better for a "little racketing when he's
green." He had always found the best fellows
were wildish once, etc.

"How's your son?" asked Sir Austin.

"O, Lipscombe's always the same," replies
the gouty advocate of wild oats. "He's quiet—
that's one good thing; but there's no getting
the country to take him, so I must give up
hopes of that."

Lord Lipscombe entering the room just
then, Sir Austin surveyed him, and was not
astonished at the refusal of the country to take
him.

"Wild oats! wild oats!" again thinks the
baronet, as he contemplates the headless, de-
generate, weedy issue and result.

He was content to remark that he thought
the third generation of wild oats would be a
pretty thin crop.

The Ordeal of Richard Feverel is a great
book because it is a profoundly wise book.
The wise books of the world, the books which
embalm the deepest lessons of experience and
thus attain to a sort of sacred value, are few,
and thus become of necessity the classics of
literature. This is such a book, and it is not
only wise but witty, and is throughout executed in Mr. Meredith's most brilliant manner.
There are sayings in it which cannot be forgotten: they are as memorable as the sayings
of Gautama or Confucius, of Marcus Aurelius
or Augustine, and might be the fit texts for
great sermons.

Take, at random, some half a dozen sentences from that half-tragic note-book of Sir
Austin's, *The Pilgrim's Scrip*, a book in which
every record has the diamond's worth and
luster, and, let us hope, the diamond's unchang-
ing endurance, too.

How profoundly religious are these aphorisms:

" Expediency is man's wisdom. Doing right
is God's."

" Until he has had some deep sorrow he
will not find the divine want of prayer."

"Who rises from prayer a better man, his prayer is answered."

"For this reason so many fall from God who have attained to him, that they cling to him with their weakness, not with their strength."

And how keenly do these cut:

"Nature is not all dust. Through nature only can we ascend. St. Simeon saw the Hog in Nature, and took Nature for the Hog."

"It is the tendency of very fast people to grow organically downward."

"O, women, who like and will have for hero a rake! how soon are you not to learn that you have taken bankrupts to your bosoms, and that the putrescent gold that attracted you is the slime of the Lake of Sin!"

Or, to conclude with three that touch a sunnier height:

"The compensation for injustice is that in the darkest ordeal we gather the worthiest round us."

"There is for the mind but one grasp of happiness; from that uppermost pinnacle of wisdom, whence we see that this world is well designed."

And this most perfect of lovers' petitions:

"Give me purity to be worthy the good in her, and grant her patience to reach the good in me."

And these are but the chance gleanings of a book which it has taken all these years to lift into even moderate eminence, and which beyond its wisdom and its humor has every quality of art and genius which can make a novel great. The one consolation in the remembrance is that in this long ordeal of injustice George Meredith has not failed to gather the worthiest round him.

To catalogue qualities and speak of pathos, humor, and imagination, and make quotations is an easy task, but one feels that after all it amounts to little. The real greatness of George Meredith lies in something deeper and more inclusive; it is that he is a great poet who has chosen chiefly to work in prose. His poetic force is behind all he writes; it is the animating soul of all. It is perpetually thrusting aside the heavy garments of prose and flashing out upon us in thought and phrases which startle and fascinate us as only poetry can. How exquisite is that whole picture of Rich-

ard reading the diary of the dead Clare, with
its secrecies of unconfessed affection, its pathetic humbleness, its meek reproach! " He
could not read for tears. It was midnight.
The hour seemed to belong to her. The awful stillness and the darkness were Clare's.
Clare Doria Forey! He knew the music of
that name. *It sounded faint and mellow now
behind the hills of death.*" Is not this poetry,
too—" He pronounced love a little modestly,
as it were, a blush in his voice?"

When Sandra's song is finished the stillness
settles back again "like one folding up a precious jewel." And where are there any passages in the whole realm of fiction so full of
lyric rapture, so intoxicating in their charm of
perfect beauty, as those which describe the first
waking of love in Richard Feverel? George
Meredith's greatest moments are in the interpretation of young love and nature, and here
he does both.

"The little sky-lark went up above her, all
song, to the smooth southern cloud lying along
the blue; from a dewy copse standing dark
over her nodding hat the blackbird flitted,
calling to her with thrice mellow note; the

kingfisher flashed emerald out of the green
osiers; a bow-winged heron traveled aloft,
seeking solitude; a boat slipped toward her
containing a dreamy youth."

.   .   .   .   .   .

"Stiller and stiller grew nature, as at the
meeting of two electric clouds."

.   .   .   .   .   .

"To-morrow this place will have a memory
—the river and the meadow, and the white
falling weir. His heart will build a temple
here, and the skylark will be its high-priest
and the old blackbird its glossy-gowned chor-
ister, and there will be a sacred repast of dew-
berries. . . .

"Golden lie the meadows, golden run the
streams, red gold is on the pine-stems. The
sun is coming down to earth, and walks the
fields and the waters.

"The sun is coming down to earth, and the
fields and the waters shout to him golden
shouts. He comes, and his heralds run before
him and touch the leaves of oaks and planes
and beeches lucid green, and the pine-stems
redder gold, leaving brightest footsteps upon
thickly weeded banks, where the foxglove's

last upper-bells incline, and bramble shoots wander amid moist rich herbage."

.   .   .   .   .   .

"For this is the home of enchantment. Here, secluded from vexed shores, the prince and princess of the island meet; here, like darkling nightingales, they sit, and into eyes and ears and hands pour endless ever-fresh treasures of their souls."

.   .   .   .   .   .

"Out in the world there, on the skirts of the woodland, a sheep-boy pipes to meditative eve on a penny whistle. Love's musical instrument is as old, and as poor; it has but two stops, and yet you see the cunning musician does thus much with it."

.   .   .   .   .   .

"The tide of color has ebbed from the upper sky. In the west the sea of sunken fire draws back, and the stars leap forth and tremble and retire before the advancing moon, who slips the silver train of cloud from her shoulders, and with her foot upon the pine-tops surveys heaven.

"Young as when she looked upon the lovers in paradise, the fair Immortal journeys onward.

Fronting her it is not night, but veiled day. Full half the sky is flushed. Not darkness; not day; but the nuptials of the two.

" A soft beam travels to the fern covert under the pine-wood where they sit, and for answer . he has her eyes—turned to him an instant, timidly fluttering over the depths of his, and then downcast; for through her eyes her soul is naked to him.

" ' Lucy! my bride! my life!'

" The night-jar spins his dark monotony on the branch of the pine. The soft beam travels round them and listens to their hearts. Their lips are locked.

" Pipe no more, Love, for a time! Pipe as you will, you cannot express their first kiss; nothing of its sweetness, and of the sacredness of it nothing. St. Cecilia up aloft, before the silver organ-pipes of paradise, pressing fingers upon all the notes of which Love is but one, from her you may hear it."

Much more might be said, but here it becomes necessary to obey the limits of space, since this is an essay and not a treatise. The women - characters of George Meredith are worthy of an essay to themselves. They are

intensely living, and intensely human.   It was
one of Lord Byron's fads to pretend disgust
at seeing women eat.   It has been well said of
George Meredith's women that they eat and
are not ashamed.   Woman is to him no sentimental abstraction, no impossible deity; it delights him to show us that she is flesh and
blood, and none the worse for it; that in intellectual power she is mate of man, and in moral
power his superior, because she lives closer to
the heart of nature; that in fact the angel is as
false a description as the animal, and that in
any case the correcter our estimate of her the
higher will be her honor.   He will have nothing
to do with the doctrine that woman is but
"undeveloped man," and he roundly denounces
it as a lie.   The masculine and feminine are
forever different in scope, sphere, and essence; yet men "who have the woman in
them without being womanized are the pick
of men.   And the choicest women are those
who yield not a feather of their womanliness
for some amount of manlike strength—man's
brain, woman's heart."   She needs no spurious
daintiness to recommend her.   Let her come
to us in native naturalness, and she will save

us; for "women have us back to the conditions of primitive man, or they shoot us higher
than the topmost star." Again and again
does George Meredith insist, as Mr. Le Gal-
lienne admirably puts it, that "a man's relations to woman, how he regards her, how he
acts toward her, are the most significant things
about him." And for the man who misap-
prehends or misuses her there is tragic venge-
ance; "for women are not the end but the
means of life, and they punish us for so per-
verting their uses. They punish society." But
this theme can only be indicated, not elab-
orated.

The chief thing, from the moral point of
view, which fills the mind after a thorough perusal of George Meredith's works is their robust hopefulness. He has gone down to the
sources of life; he has uncovered its worst secrets; he has surprised the unsuspected and
dragged into light the ignored elements of conduct; he has been utterly true in his fealty to
"sacred reality," but he has retained, in and
through all, his geniality, his faith in God and
man, his hope for the world. He has told us
that the only chance of happiness is the belief

that this world is well designed, and this is his
own belief; and he adds through the lips of his
Diana of the Crossways, "*Who can really think
and not think hopefully?*" Like so many of
his aphorisms, this is one that goes to the root
of things and expresses a philosophy. It would
seem to teach that pessimism is the disease
of shallow minds, a surface complaint which
attacks mainly the less forceful and efficient
natures of the race; the wider and deeper
natures have too strong a vitality to be its victims. Go deep enough, he says, and you will
find that the sources of hope and vital joy are
not dried up. You will find the world on the
whole well designed. You will find no chaos,
but a most Divine Kosmos, to know which is
to rejoice in life. Despair is a disease; the
sane and sound nature must needs be hopeful.
A little thought, like a little knowledge, is a
dangerous thing, and may breed pessimism.
A little more thought takes one out of the
storm-belt into the far-reaching sunlight. "*I
think it al'ays the plan in a diclemmer,*" says
the wise Mrs. Berry, "*to pray God and walk
forward.*" Nor can any better plan be invented for the guidance of bewildered souls.

13

There is, of course, a thoughtless optimism, as
there is a thoughtless pessimism—the optimism of those who recognize no problems or
dilemmas in life, and whose gayety is the mere
frisking ebullience of the happy animal. But
the glory of George Meredith's optimism is
that having seen the worst he believes in the
best. Having touched the lowest depth, he
has still had eyes to discover the starry height,
and has had ears to hear the music of the
spheres. In this resolute and intelligent optimism he and Robert Browning once more
find themselves akin; nor can I better express
the spirit of Meredith's work than by putting
into his lips the well-known verse of Browning:

"I have gone the whole round of creation: I saw and I
    spoke;
I, a work of God's hand for that purpose, received in my
    brain
And pronounced on the rest of his handwork—returned him
    again
His creation's approval or censure: I spoke as I saw,
I report as a man may on God's work—*all's love, yet all's
    law.*"

THE POETRY OF DESPAIR.

MATTHEW ARNOLD AND JAMES THOMSON (B. V.).

A LITTLE more than sixty years ago Lord Byron remarked to Medwin, in the course of those memorable conversations which passed between them at Pisa, that if a cry of blasphemy was raised against him on account of his drama of " Cain " it would be interesting to know what the Methodists at home would say to Goethe's " Faust." " What would they think of the colloquies of Mephistopheles and his pupil, or the more daring language of the Prologue, which no one will ever venture to translate ? " It is curious and significant to remember how completely this prophecy has been falsified. At the very moment when Lord Byron was telling Medwin that the Prologue would never be translated Hayward was meditating his translation, and probably no poem has been so repeatedly rendered into English, or is more widely read to-day, than

the "Faust" of Goethe. Nor can it be said
that any very violent shock was inflicted on
the susceptibilities of British taste by either
the grim pleasantry of the colloquies or the
daring breadth of the Prologue. On the contrary, the publication of his rendering of
"Faust" immediately won for Hayward attention and reputation, and those who had
clamored loudest against Byron were wholly
silent in the presence of Goethe. Nor was
this strange silence to be attributed wholly, or
indeed in any large degree, to the caprice of
opinion or public indifference ; it resulted
rather from the great revolution which had
taken place in the attitude of the age toward
subjects of faith.

In no respect is this revolution more accu-
rately reflected than in the new current of
thought and feeling which is found in the
poetry of the last half-century. It is the very
nature of the poet that his finer sympathies
should thrill with the first vibration of change,
and that he himself should be at once the her-
ald and the minister of change. He possesses
the intellectual counterpart of that intensely
sensitive physical organization which perceives

instinctively the earliest and slightest atmos-
pheric indications of breaking weather, the
moment when the summer breathes its first
sick sigh of death or the spring first stirs and
quickens in the frozen earth. Where he is absolutely true to himself and his instincts the
poet thus becomes the most authentic voice of
his age ; he condenses its spirit into concrete
utterance, he interprets its truest yearnings,
he catches the meaning of its deepest need,
and so holds the mirror up to its inmost nature that in him coming generations recognize
the true index to its character. The history
of England is the history of its poetry, because
its poetry is the quintessence of its real life.
In it the rough kindliness and valor, the shallowness and lust, the ferment and bitterness,
the confused doubt and yearning of any given
epoch find their perfect reflection ; and a perfect acquaintance with the literature of a generation will afford a more accurate idea of its
character than any narrative of parliamentary
policies or warlike strategies.

No more striking illustration of such a truth
as this can be furnished than by the entirely
new vein of poetry which may be said to have

been opened up during the last fifty years in
the direction of religious and theological problems. The beginning of the nineteenth century not merely witnessed the breaking up of
political and social life throughout Europe, but,
to a very large extent, a revolution against
formulated theology, whose first effect was a
quickened interest in the grave problems of
human destiny. Byron himself is a case in
point. The outcry against " Cain " and
" Heaven and Hell " was aroused by the free
and daring handling of such questions which
those poems contained. It was in vain that
Byron protested he had only followed in the
steps of Milton, and that Milton neither at-
tended divine service nor accepted the orthodox creeds of his day. It was instinctively
felt that the fermenting leaven of an entirely
new religious movement was at work in the
mystery-plays of Byron. They were not the
work of a great poetic artist who had found
his inspiration in the " Paradise Lost," but the
outcry of a living man in whom the spirit of
the age was speaking, and who was inspired
by the restless misery of religious doubt. The
same spirit animated Shelley, whose professed

atheism was a mere form which masked the uncontrollable yearnings of one who

> " Stood between two worlds, one dead,
> The other powerless to be born."

The Tractarian movement of 1830 presaged and hastened the culmination of this unsettlement in belief, and, by proposing the Church as the one authority in faith, practically split the world of thought into two hostile camps. From that moment theological problems have had a paramount interest in English thought, and have deeply colored the whole course of modern literature, and most of all modern poetry. For the first time controversial points of faith, speculation, doubt, and despair have afforded themes for poets. Arthur Hugh Clough, who describes himself as for a long while drawn like a straw up the draught of a chimney by the force of the Oxford movement, came out of it completely lamed and wrecked, and uttered the wail of thousands when he wrote :

> " O, might we for assurance' sake
> Some arbitrary judgment take,
> And willfully pronounce it true."

The " Festus " of Bailey was charged to the

very brim with the like unrest and heart-
wearied yearning. The melodious languors of
Tennyson's early poems soon gave way to the
deep-centered activities of thought which were
every-where rending men's lives apart, and the
golden clime in which the poet was born was
speedily vexed with the rolling cloud and tempest of the great upheaval. The " In Memoriam " is the nineteenth century's Book of
Job, and is inseparably inwoven with the history of the century because it is woven out of
the sentiment of the century. The best poetry
which Matthew Arnold has written is saturated
with the same sentiment, but in its weariness
is the saddest of all the lyrical cries which
have pierced the times. In Robert Browning,
above all, the movement has found its climax,
for no English poet has so consistently used
poetry as the vehicle of theological speculation,
and few out of darkness and perplexity have
sung so high and clear a song.

Together with the effect of the religious
movement on poetry we have to take into
consideration the character of modern life in
itself. Is there any thoughtful man who is not
conscious of the enormous overstrain, the fever-

ish and almost diseased activity which competition of all kinds has imported into human life? One of our poets has painted his vision of the world as seen from some point of central calm:

> " Like a vast wheel that spins through humming air,
>   And time, life, death, are sucked within its breath,
> And thrones and kingdoms like sere leaves are hurled
>   Down to its maelstrom ; for its wind of death
> Sweeps the wide skies, and shakes the flaring suns,
> So fast the wheel spins, and the glory runs."

Might not the immense whirl and speed of modern life be represented as the blind spinning of a huge wheel, or a maelstrom sending forth deep thunder, into whose fatal circles life, and all that is best in life, are being rapidly swept? It is Matthew Arnold who tells us of the two desires that toss about the poet's blood :

> "One drives him to the world without,
>   And one to solitude."

But where is this healing solitude? Or how indeed can the simple tastes which thrive best in its seclusion and its silence be preserved amid the growth of cities, the haste to be rich, the competition of trade, the pressure and overstrain to which it seems inevitable that all classes of society must submit in this day of

ours? Here there is a double process, producing more and more with each decade that
note of deep despair which is now beginning
to be apparent in poetry. On the one hand
we have the wide disturbance of faith, producing confusion and sterility in poetry; on the
other hand we have the diseased activity of
modern life communicating itself to literature
and revenging itself in that cry of hopeless
weariness and incommunicable sadness which
is almost the foremost, and certainly the most
distressing, quality of modern poetry. It is
one of the axioms of pessimism that "development of culture is development of sorrow,"
and indeed, finally, that all things lead up to
the transcendental misery of the Absolute himself. Is this the grim goal toward which
modern poetry is drifting? Is culture without
faith proving itself only the development of
sorrow, and are we thus being led through
agnosticism to despair?

It has been said that poetry is faith, and
though something of accuracy may have been
sacrificed to the exigences of epigram, yet we
may accept the definition as at least high and
noble. Without faith no man shall see God,

and without that vision of God no poet can accomplish aught of noble or divine. He must make his life a poem, he must live ever as in his great Task-master's eye. Whoever else may be disquieted in vain, he who sings must know in whom he has believed. I have shown that the greatest periods of English poetry have been the periods of religious faith; it is worth pondering that the earliest forms of poetry are essentially religious. Have we forgotten this unalterable relation between poetry and religion? Have we forgotten the rock from which were hewn the noblest forms of poetry, the trees of life whose leaves have been for the healing of the nations? Or at least, it may be urged, have we invented, or discovered, or evolved any poetic ideal half so noble as this that lives forever in the stern and simple speech of Milton? It is quite certain that he who forgets these things forgets the things that are for his peace. The greatest poets are unanimous against him. The minstrel strikes deep heart-notes because he has high visions; the mightiest singers have been made mighty by their faith. He cannot weave imperishable singing raiment from the broken woofs of faithlessness; he cannot pour the poet's highest music, nor any music other than a discord or a wail, through the thin reed of contemporary agnosticism. For the highest art calmness and sanity of spirit are needed; indeed, these are its most stringent and unalterable conditions. There must be unity of thought in the poet; there must be a divine center round which the thought may gather. If it be otherwise, if there be nothing true and nothing sure, if the blood is always at fever-heat and the thought in a perpetual flux, what song he shall sing will have at best only the piercing sweetness and sad incoherence of a snatch of music sung by wild lips in a delirium. For the strenuous and abiding tasks of the highest art, for a " Paradise Lost " or an " Excursion," the mind will have no vigor and impulse of sustained effort. And it was this that Shelley felt when he wrote to Godwin: " I cannot but be conscious, in much of what I write, of an absence of that tranquillity which is the attribute and accompaniment of power." It is this which is felt and unwittingly confessed by the poets of our own day. They are too far removed from a secure basis

of faith, and too much disturbed by the fierce
haste of life, to possess that tranquillity which
is the attribute and accompaniment of power.
How, indeed, can tranquillity be the possession
of men whose confession rather than whose
creed is: " Here we drift, like white sail across
the wild ocean, now bright on the wave, now
darkling in the trough of the sea.   But from
what port did we sail?   Who knows?   Or to
what port are we bound?   Who knows?   There
is no one to tell us but such poor weather-
tossed mariners as ourselves, whom we speak
as we pass. . . . But what know they more
than we?"

There is another element which has contrib-
uted to the creation of a poetry of despair,
namely, the failure of modern culture as a
substitute for religious faith.   Here pessimism
comes much nearer the truth than positivism, for
Hartmann, in his *Phänomenologie des sittlichen
Bewusstseins*, shows that the augmentation of
happiness by culture has been "dearly purchased by an overwhelmingly greater amount
of sorrow, necessarily called into being by the
process."   It has been said that culture
has "invaded even the nurseries of young

children ; and the culturists rejoice at the
sight of crowds of little wretches, of eight
years old and under, cramming for competitive
examinations." At all events, it is true enough
that the zeal for culture, either in the limited
sense of these passages, or in the larger meaning of the word, has become a devouring passion in the late decades of the nineteenth
century. Now, no one will doubt that there is
a broad and noble culture perfectly consonant
with a devout and spiritual faith. In point of
fact there can be no breadth or nobility in a
culture which does not include the spirit and
the character as well as the intellect. Such
culture is not purchased by an overwhelmingly
greater amount of sorrow ; rather it adds
"sunshine to daylight," it completes and en-
larges the circle of being, it is the golden stair
up which men climb to a place but little lower
than the angels. But this is not the culture
of which Hartmann speaks ; it is not the culture
whose arrogant and self-sufficient spirit breathes
in our literature to-day. Modern culture knows
nothing of a place a little lower than the
angels ; it dismisses with contempt what it
chooses to call unverifiable beliefs ; it has no

spiritual vision, and is the antagonist rather than the handmaiden of faith.   It has endeavored to fill a part too vast for its powers, by substituting itself for faith, and it has failed. Could the result be otherwise?   What does culture without faith do but create with each step in its progress fresh needs, and so aggravate its thirst and multiply its sorrows— surely, in a very striking sense, the sorrows of those that seek after a strange God? For the experiment is not new; it has been made many times, and once at least, on a scale of unparalleled tragedy, by a certain king who was wisest among men, and a great poet withal, who had houses and treasure more than all they that had been before him in Jerusalem, and had delights of knowledge, and of art, and of pleasure, and knew wisdom and madness and folly, and so came at last to say that all was vanity, and the one supreme peace and wisdom was found in the remembering of the Creator.   But the lesson has not yet sunk deep into the ears of his generation; and so the failure of culture as a substitute for religious faith has worked like a bitter leaven in the poetry of the age, and has produced despair.

Let us turn to Matthew Arnold again. His
poetry is virtually the confession that his culture has failed. In him the personal note is
supreme; it is the problem of his own life
which fascinates us. He can strike chords of
great power and sweetness, and sometimes
of deep tenderness, but he is greatest as a poet
when he expresses his own heartfelt mournful-
ness and yearning. The two worlds he stands
between are the old world of faith which is
dead, and the new world of culture which is
"powerless to be born." He cannot hide his
sorrow, it is ever before him; he cannot dis-
guise the fact that his culture has failed to
satisfy him. He cries with an exceeding bitter
cry after that cross which he has declared a
vanished myth and that assured creed which
he has dismissed as a beautiful imposture. He
confesses the cruel conflict that is within him,
the devoutness which has survived his doubts,
the religious yearnings which are not quenched
by his denials. In this respect his position is
unique ; he sings as one believing in his unbe-
lief, and he is only saved from utter despair by
this devoutness which he has not dared to
destroy. But beyond that the most memora-

ble feature of his poetry is its acknowledg-
ment—wrung from him rather than confessed
—that his lack of faith has sapped the very
courses of his thought, and that culture in its
utmost beauty and refinement has proved
itself but shifting sand when the storms have
beaten and the winds of trouble blown. He
sees with dismay and despair the hopeless tangle
of the age, and is as one without hope. He is
smitten with the intellectual fever of the times,
and cries:

> " What shelter to grow ripe is ours,
> What leisure to grow wise ? "

The failure of faith, the failure of culture,
the unrest and haste of life, find perfect
expression in his pages ; for he is too true a
poet, and too real a man, not to deal sincerely
with those to whom he appeals. And so the
music of his speech, in spite of its exquisite
charm and tenderness, deepens more and more
into the lyric wail of immeasurable distress,
and it is with wistful yearning he looks back to
the stronger poets of the past, and cries:

> " Too fast we live, too much are tried,
> Too harassed to attain
> Wordsworth's sweet calm, or Goethe's wide
> And luminous view to gain."

14

That is to say, he has not the impassivity and selfishness of Goethe, which makes mere personal culture an all-sufficing purpose; and still less has he the undisturbed and simple faith of Wordsworth, which makes tranquillity a natural consequence.

And since Matthew Arnold himself has pointed us to Wordsworth, and indicated him as one of the only two who in our troubled day have attained "to see their way," it may be well to ask what preserved Wordsworth from the disease of pessimism, which had already tainted English poetry, while he lived and thought? How was it that amid the fever of the age he continued to live—to quote his own exquisite words—

> "With heart as calm as lakes that sleep,
> In frosty moonlight glistening;
> Or mountain rivers where they creep
> Along a channel smooth and deep
> To their own far-off murmurs listening."

It was because he preserved his faith in God, his simple tastes, his love of nature. He was content to lose his life that he might save it; or, in other words, to be true to the things unseen and eternal at whatever sacrifice of the things seen and temporal. It may be that he provokes ridicule by his occasional triviality of theme; but this is one of the penalties of fame —that the tares are bound up with the wheat of genius, and that the shallow and the unwise will never learn how to discriminate between them.   It may be true that the more turbulent and volcanic passions of human nature find no reflection in his writings; but the nobler aspects of human destiny continually absorb him, and in this the poet has chosen that " better part " which shall make his best poetry immortal.   What he has succeeded in doing is the rare and difficult task of uniting the Christian and the philosophic genius in poetry which, at its best, is full of charm, simplicity, and sublimity.   He has preserved that faith in God which is the secret of all tranquillity, and without which the greatest poetry cannot be.   He has turned aside with a noble disdain from the strifes of secular ambition, the greed for gold, the race for fame, and so has preserved " the harvest of a quiet eye," and found that

> " Impulses of deeper birth
> Have come to him in solitude."

And because he did this he also preserved the clearness and sanity of his spirit; he was kept

in peace, he was tainted with no morbid dis-
quietudes; he sang no dirges of despair, but
a sweet high strain of purest song which has
been for the healing and the inspiration of his
country, and which will endure in gathered
power when the bitter cries of our modern
singers are lost in oblivion or are remembered
only with sorrowful disdain. Just as Milton
has been pictured standing like a colossal
statue of Apollo, watching the arrow-flight of
his immortal song, while round his feet, unconscious of his presence, dance the wine-stained
satyrs of the court of Charles, so we may figure
Wordsworth standing on the threshold of this
perturbed generation of ours, clothed in his
simplicity, rebuking its fretful strife with his
serenity and its despairing voices with his
faith.

How far we have removed from Wordsworth, and how foreign the spirit of our later
poetry is to the spirit which animated his,
we can judge by one of the latest contributions
made to our literature, the poetry of James
Thomson, long known as " B. V." In the
" City of Dreadful Night" despair has reached
its apotheosis. The ultimatum of pessimism is

universal suicide, and that is precisely the doctrine propounded in this remarkable poem. I will not attempt to determine with critical dogmatism the position of Thomson as a poet; it would be easy to exaggerate or underrate his importance; but the significance of such a poem, dedicated to Leopardi, approved by George Eliot, widely read, full of

> " Infections of unutterable sadness,
> Infections of incalculable madness,
> Infections of incurable despair,"

it is at least well to indicate.   And the significance of Thomson's poetry is that it pushes to logical fulfillment those conditions of religious disturbance and intellectual unrest which we have already noted.   Here, at last, is a man too high-minded to chant the praises of the "Goddess of Lubricity" because he has lost religious assurance, and too terribly sincere to be content with mere wailings of regret for a faith whose poetry fascinates him, but whose authenticity he derides; he therefore strikes the iron harp-string of the completest pessimism, and not merely announces his conclusion that life is not worth living, but that it ought not to be preserved.

When Thomson called the "City of Dreadful Night " an atheistical poem he spoke with a perfect appreciation of its scope and purpose. There could be no other word for a poem whose climax of horror is found in the picture of that black-draped cathedral crowded with human shadows, with its swart preacher whose eyes burn beneath his somber cowl, proclaiming as the best of all good tidings:

> " O, brothers of sad lives ! that are so brief,
> A few short years must bring us all relief,
> Can we not bear these years of laboring breath ?
> But if you would not this poor life fulfill,
> Lo, you are free to end it when you will,
> Without the fear of waking after death."

But Thomson is, nevertheless, a memorable example of how difficult and even impossible it is to construct poetry out, of pure negation. We are reminded of the caustic epigram of Voltaire, that if God did not exist we should be obliged to invent him, and of the saying of Coleridge, that a poet is always a religious man. In spite of all avowed atheism Thomson finds himself writing in fierce condemnation of—

> " The poets who sing their own lusts
> Instead of the hymns of the Lord,"

and declaring with more of a prophet's fervor
than a pessimist's stoicism—

> " No wealth can bribe away the doom of the living God ;
> No haughtiest strength confront the sway of his chastening
> rod."

God refuses to be exiled from the heart,
though shut out from the brain of the poet;
and ever and again a gush of pure faith, like
the song of a thrush heard between the thun-
der-claps of a dying storm, rises through the
darkness of his despair. Especially is this the
case when his stormy anguish of revolt against
social and theological order gives place to the
sadness of personal regret. His eyes then fill
with tears when looking on life's autumn fields
and thinking of the days that are no more.
With inimitable pathos, and scarcely less inimitable daring, he recalls the one spirit he
loved upon earth; and, as in the poem of
" Vane's Dream," alternately thrills the reader
with his tenderness and offends him with his
coarse realism. And, indeed, in this respect,
Thomson resembles Heine, for whom he entertained a deep affection, and from whom he has
manifestly caught inspiration. His satire and
tenderness follow each other with swift strokes ;

the secret of his own life-long agony is often
guarded by a spirit of mocking laughter, and
when we least expect it a turn of the page flashes
sudden sunlight through the gloom. As with
Heine so with him, there is often something
sadder in his laughter than his weeping, and his
very irony pains us with suggestions of the tears
that are behind it. We know while we read
many poets that their sweetest songs spring
from saddest thought; that, like the Pot of
Basil, celebrated in Boccaccio's story and
Keats's poem, the sweet bloom and foliage
which astonish Florence owe their fullness to
the secret death that lies below. But in
Thomson the sense of pain often becomes
overmastering; and, for pity's sake, we pray
to hear no more. It must ever be a startling
paradox that such bitterness and pathos, such
denial and faith, can exist in the same nature;
that the " Mater Tenebrarum," whose cry after
the dead is worthy of comparison with Burns's
wail to his " Mary in Heaven," should be written by the same hand as " The Doom of a
City," and " The City of Dreadful Night."

It would be interesting to point out how
Thomson, without being imitative, occasion-

ally can almost rival Shelley and surpass Blake
upon their own ground. In such poems as
" The Naked Goddess," with its mysterious
symbolism and spiritual reticence, and " Virtue
and Vice," with the satiric simplicity of its
short and epigrammatic lines, Thomson has
caught the very spirit of Blake's method and
utterance. In his longest poems the influence
of Shelley is unmistakable, and it is a grave
error of judgment that the editor of the posthumous volume should have omitted Thomson's
poem on Shelley, which could not but be of
biographic interest at least, and have included
such clever rubbish as " The Pilgrimage of St.
Nicotine," which was only written to sell. In
the love of cloud-scenery, and the faithful
painting of it ; in all those large effects of
weirdness and solemnity which make sunrises
and sunsets so full of awe and mystery ; in the
poetry of wonder and desolation, Thomson is
a master, and he has studied Shelley to good
purpose. Shelley himself has not painted a
sunset with a finer apprehension of those large
effects of light and meaning, as opposed to
those exquisite touches of minute observation,
in which Tennyson, for instance, abounds, than

has Thomson in the following extract from
"The Doom of a City:"

> " And so, at length, we entered it, and faced
> The thin, dark lines of countless masts, all traced
> Upon the saddest sunset ever seen—
> Spread out like an interminable waste
> Of red and saffron sand, devoured by slow
> Persistent fire ; beneath whose desolate glow
> A city lay—thick-zoned with solemn green
> Of foliage massed upon the steeps around.
> Between those mast-lines flamed the crystal fires
> Of multitudinous windows, and on high
> Grand marble palaces and temples, crowned
> With golden domes and radiant towers and spires,
> Stood all entranced beneath that desert sky,
> Based on an awful stillness."

But Thomson has sufficient original force
to stand by himself, and to be judged alone.
What that judgment will be it is of course
difficult to predict. But if it be a true axiom
of criticism that a poet's greatness is in precise
proportion to his power in pure imagination,
then he must take a very high place in contemporary poetry. The greatest master of
the poetry of pure wonder which English literature has ever had is undoubtedly Coleridge.
There is a subtle charm and magic, a witchery
of sound and vision, in such poems as " Khubla
Khan " and " Christabel " which has never been

approached by any other English poet; and
"The Ancient Mariner" still remains the most
splendid effort of pure imaginative poetry in
modern literature.   There has, indeed, been an
attempt to claim for Keats the place next to
Coleridge in the poetry of wonder, on the
strength of his fragment called "The Eve of St.
Mark's," and his single ballad "La Belle Dame
sans Merci."   But we fail entirely to perceive
any indications in either of these poems of that
clear and vivid faculty of intense imagination
which is indispensable in romantic or super-
natural poetry.   The second place must clearly
be assigned to Dante Gabriel Rossetti, whose
"Blessed Damozel," whether considered in itself according to its qualities of intense passion,
spirituality, and imaginativeness, or as the work
of a youth of eighteen, may be said to stand
alone in modern poetry.   And after these two,
at a great distance, and as a poet of wholly
different temper and method, we should be
compelled to name James Thomson.   Com-
pared with either Coleridge or Rossetti he
falls very short in the qualities where they are
supreme; but he possesses an imaginative intensity, a Dantesque power of vision, and a

mastery over the imagery of gloom and fear, which is a distinct and rare endowment. At his word magic curtains of inwoven darkness rush down out of the brightest heavens, and every chord of sense vibrates with secret dread. Let any one read such a poem as "In the Room," with its dreadful realism and gradual terror, or the poem called "Insomnia" in the posthumous volume, and he will know what we mean. The vision we see through the eyes of the sleepless man—and here the sufferer was Thomson himself—of the slant moonlight on the ceiling thrown, mixed with the faint and broken lamp-gleam; the Hours standing one by one at the bed's foot, each one—

> "Still, as a pillar of basaltic stone,
> And all enveloped in a somber shroud,
> Except the wan face, drooping, heavy-browed;"

and the weary space between the tolling bells, like an awful desert to be crossed in fear and pain—has the distinctness and the haunting memory of nightmare. And here, as in "The City of Dreadful Night," he proves himself a master of meter and of a sort of deep, in-toned, inward music, like the heavy rise and fall of immense seas, which is perhaps the

secret of the indefinable charm which lures us
on in spite of our aversion.

Thomson has spoken in "The Doom of a
City" of the mysteriousness of his own life,
and has said :

" The chords of sympathy, which should have bound me
    In sweet communion with earth's brotherhood
I drew in tight and tighter still around me,
    Strangling my best existence for a mood."

The implication is that he was not unconscious
of that growth of melancholy which shrouded
his whole life in gloom, and that he deplored
it. At times, too, he must have overcome it.
There are times when the very spirit of joy
sings through his lips and his verse has the
swift rush and sweetness of a bird's song. He
possessed lyrical power of no common order,
and had the rare faculty of writing songs
which sing themselves to their own music.
And in one lovely poem in his last volume, entitled " He Heard Her Sing," he manifests a sustained power and volume of lyrical sweetness
such as it would be hard to match among any of
the younger writers of the day. No more im-
passioned song of love and spring has ever been
sung in our times ; and this poem alone would

stamp Thomson as a poet of very high order.
But such moods are rare, and are all too brief.
They are signs of what he might have done
had his life been happier, and had that mood,
of which he speaks, not tightened round him
its strangling death-cord; as it is he stands in
modern literature like his own vision of the
sleepless hour—

> "Still, as a pillar of basaltic stone,
> And all enveloped in a somber shroud."

Here then is the acutest form of that faithlessness which is the malady of the age; here
is its latest and, let us hope, its ultimate development. Thomson has produced and be-
queathed to the world a genuine poetry of
despair, which in power, splendor, and earnestness is entirely unique. We emphasize its
perfect genuineness because it is not to be
confounded for a moment with that fashionable
poetic agnosticism which appears unto men
to fast, and is never so happy as when per-
suading every body else that it is exquisitely
miserable. Thomson's poetry is too terribly
sincere, and its profound gloom and bitterness
are too manifestly the product of despair in its
most forlorn and hopeless phase. The bound-

ary of doubt is long since left behind, and the
city of dreadful night which he has reached is
the realm of pure negation.   It might be said
in defense of what Tennyson has called honest
doubt that the sincere questioning of accepted formulæ is not without service to the
cause of truth.   Had Galileo never doubted
the scientific deductions of his day, nor Co-
lumbus the accepted geography, nor Luther
the conventional dogmas of the Church, the
world might have gone on for another century
or two without a true astronomy, an America,
or a Reformation.   Such skepticism doubts its
way toward certainty, and comes at length to
find a stronger faith its own.   But Thomson
is not one of the great world-teachers who,
"fired with burning sense of God and right,"
doubts men's doubts away.   He is a man who
has broken down in the quest, who has sought
the Holy Grail in vain, who at last, hopeless
of seeing any divine light "starlike mingle
with the stars," has laid himself down in the
unending forest, and is choked with the thick
drift of darkness which every way falls upon
him like the black snow of death.   He has no
questions to put to the oracle of doom; he

has received his answer, and here records his
belief that life is

> " Darkness at the core,
> And dust and ashes all that is."

The accent of regret, which makes the poetry
of Arnold so pathetic in the very calmness of
its hopelessness, is almost wanting.   Thomson
does not tell us how

> " The sea of faith
> Was once, too, at the full, and round earth's shore
> Lay like the folds of a bright girdle furled ;
>   But now I only hear
> Its melancholy long-withdrawing roar,
>   Retreating to the breath
> Of the night-wind down the vast edges drear
>   And naked shingles of the world."

Regret is a still sad music, whose key-note is
plaintiveness; but the predominating quality
in Thomson's verse is a sort of sonorous
thunder, an awful and majestic music, which
might aptly be likened to the long-withdraw-
ing roar of breakers on the naked shingles of
the world, when the mood of ocean is mighty
rather than melancholy.

In one brief poem, entitled " A Recusant,"
he has indeed touched a tender and regretful
chord, and, looking at the church-spire " lifted

mysterious through the twilight glooms," has
cried :

> " How sweet to enter in, to kneel and pray
> With all the others whom we love so well,
> All disbelief and doubt might pass away,
> All peace float to us with its Sabbath bell."

But this is a rare and casual mood, a moment
of tenderness after long weeping, which in nowise represents his habitual thought.   For
equally wanting in him is that accent of forlorn faith which every-where quivers through
the conflict of the " In Memoriam," and rises
to its sublimest utterance in the famous fifty-
fifth section, where the believing but bewildered doubter cries :

> " I falter where I firmly trod,
> And fall with all my weight of cares
> Upon the world's great altar-stairs
> Which slope through darkness up to God."

For him there are no sloping altar-stairs gleaming upward through the darkness, and the
darkness is impenetrable and past all hope of
morning.   He himself, as we have shown,
clearly apprehended and rightly described the
purpose of his most remarkable poem, when
he called " The City of Dreadful Night" an
atheistical writing.   Those who knew him

15

best fully understood the completeness of that despair which consumed him, when they printed on his funeral card his own lines, full of the bitterest pathos and hopelessness:

> " Weary of erring in this desert life,
>   Weary of hoping hopes forever vain,
> Weary of struggling in all-sterile strife,
>   Weary of thought which maketh nothing plain,
> I close my eyes and calm my panting breath,
> And pray to thee, O, ever-quiet death !
>   To come and soothe away my bitter pain."

Thomson may be described as the Poe of English poetry, and in many respects there is a singular likeness between the two men. Both were lonely and embittered, both knew the early loss of love, both chose to dwell on the weird borderland of imaginative terror, both were victims of intemperance, both died in hospital, and both were smitten with the same immeasurable hopelessness.

It may be added that in both Poe and Thomson there is not merely the same distinction of style, the same power of melody and vein of weirdness, but the same remoteness and intangibility of theme. It might easily be shown, and as regards Thomson it is obvious enough, that it is quite possible for a poet

to be at once a master of realism and super-
naturalism ; but in both poets the supernatural-
ism is in excess.   For this reason neither will
ever appeal to mankind at large.   It is the fault
and almost the disease of modern poets that
they perplex themselves to discover abstruse
themes, and recondite fragments of history, as
proper subjects for the exercise of their art,
when in truth the finest of all themes for
poetry, like the flowers, lie at their very feet, in
the actual human life which beats its music
out around them.   Judging Thomson from a
purely critical stand-point, we are bound to own
that his poetry will assuredly suffer at the
hands of time through this defect of theme;
although, on the other hand, it may be said
that the personal interest which attaches to
all that he has written will do much to allure
those whom his remoteness will repel.

There, however, likeness between Poe and
Thomson ceases and difference begins. Thomson has none of Poe's heartless insincerity.
He does not trade in anguish. He is utterly
incapable of the vanity Poe manifested when
he strove to prove the music of his " Raven "
a mere artistic trick, and, by inference,

his despair a mere histrionic feat. Moreover,
while Poe is simply a meteoric genius, a wandering star, a man cursed and ruined by his
own follies, and without significance as regards
his times, Thomson's great claim to notice is
the fact that he is a portent, full of grave significance to those who study the character of
the times in the character of their literature.
He began his lessons in pessimism while a
mere lad under the tuition of Mr. Charles
Bradlaugh ; he graduated in despair under the
life-long influences of secularism. Poverty and
misfortune may have had much to do with the
souring of his nature and the ruin of his life.
But there have been many men of loftier
genius than his who have borne the full weight
of both, and have come out of the discipline of
sorrow not merely chastened, but strengthened.
He himself has sung in praise of William
Blake, the poet-painter, who

> " Came to the desert of London town,
>   Mirk miles broad ;
> He wandered up, and he wandered down,
>   Ever alone with God."

Did he remember while he wrote the poem
that the man he praised never earned more

than daily bread during all his long hard life, and yet died singing rapturous hymns? Did he remember how men before and after Blake's time had borne the same slings and arrows of outrageous fortune? how Samuel Johnson had taken fifteenpence for a day's work in literature, and Goldsmith had drudged in Grub Street all his life, and Carlyle had lived and thought on oatmeal for many a month in a Scotch garret, and yet had none of them cursed God and died?

It was not the misfortune and hardship of Thomson's life which produced his pessimism. Others have borne as much, and yet have come out victorious. It was because in all that desert of London town he was not alone with God ; because he had settled it with himself that " there was no hint of good " throughout the universe; because, in fact, for him there was no God, that the darkness closed down upon him while it was yet day, and out of that mist of thick blackness the only voice which reached his fellows was a voice of heart-broken misery, of complete and tragic failure.

To such a point, then, in one direction, have we come in the development of modern poetry.

Goethe in his day foresaw and foretold the growth of a "literature of despair," and his prediction is fulfilled. The causes for this perilous development I have endeavored to indicate; they are to be found in the new current of theological speculation which affected poetry in the beginning of the century, in the wide disturbance of faith which ensued, in the failure of culture as a substitute for religious faith, and, finally, in the overstrain of life which is characteristic of the times in which we live. Simplicity and sanity are qualities which have been gradually dying out of English poetry for many a year, and the morbid, the sensational, the exaggerated, have taken their places. The pages of even our greatest poets bear evidence of the influence of religious disquiet, and it is rare that the query of doubt is not stated with far greater force and effect than the rejoinder of faith. If poetry has any ministry at all in the world, if it be not a merely ornamental art, if it be at all what Milton said it was, and what Wordsworth proved it was, a gift of God, capable of great and holy service for mankind, it must be evident that we have shamefully misused the gift, or that our conception of its uses and Milton's are very different indeed. At all events, there can be no question which estimate has resulted in the noblest poetry, from whose lips has come the deathless singing. When Milton told his friends how he lay awake at night, waiting for God to touch his thoughts to music, he revealed the only source of great poetry ; for if inspiration is not given to modern seers and singers, illumination is, and from God descends every good and perfect gift. That is the lesson which we need to learn to-day. The way of reform is in the direction of Milton and Wordsworth. We must regain our lost simplicity of life, the old and fruitful discipline of "plain living and high thinking." We must refuse to barter solitude and calm for any glittering baubles which may be snatched from the fierce race of life lived at fever-heat. In a word, our poets must return to Nature, must return to God ; and when the old sweet faith grows strong again the new despair will vanish and the garments of heaviness give place to the singing-robes of praise.

For the whole secret of the restlessness and bitter thought of our times is that their moral

attitude is one of blind and arrogant revolt
against the sacred ancient order of the world.
We have scorned the limitations of human in-
telligence, as we are now scorning the very
limitations of wholesome human life itself.   It
is time we were reminded that there are points
of knowledge beyond which we may not go,
and laws of life which we dare not violate.
What shall it profit us that we have swept the
skies with our telescopes and counted the
stars of heaven on our charts if in the intoxi-
cation of our knowledge we forget that those
golden fires of night were lighted by One who
is manifold in power, and that in wisdom he
hath made them all?   It is a right proud boast
that we have beckoned the lightning and it
has come, running our errands and bearing
our messages on wings swifter than the wind;
but small gain is ours if our days are hence-
forth devoured with haste, and the stolen
fire of Jupiter becomes a perilous possession,
and is well avenged upon the hands that stole
it.   What recompense is there for the loss of
reverence? What gain is worthy to be counted
against that immense disaster which has up-
rooted the sobriety and calm of life, which has

robbed us of our leisure and destroyed the very power of contemplation? *Quest and Vision* I have ventured to call this little book, because life itself is a perpetual quest, and the noblest results of life and literature are but so many visionary glimpses into the solemn mys- tery and beauty which lie inscrutable around us and fold us like an atmosphere. But in all such quest there must be reverence, and not less there must be room for rest and silence. There must be knowledge of ignorance as well as thirst for wisdom ; space for thought as well as time for speech; bowers of greenwood where Sir Galahad may rest and pray, as well as grim wastes where the foul foe hovers and the battle waits; and the Holy Grail floats nearest when the world is hushed, and the secret of God is manifest alone to those who do his will. That divine vision is not revealed to the presumptuous pride of half-enlightened ignorance, nor to the irreverent haste of trivial and pretentious curiosity. We want, as Mrs. Browning said forty years ago, the touch of Christ's hand upon our poets, that their dead forms of art may live and that they may know how to expound "agony into renovation." But that divine hand is not upon our poets, they have not found rest unto their souls; and hence the agony of the age has been expounded, but not the renovation.

Meantime let us be sure that we are just now only pausing in an interval. The fountain of high poetry is not dried up for England. Its volume as it flows within our view is lessened and contracted, but it only runs low for a time, after the manner of intermittent springs. Even now under ground—unknown as yet by us—it may be gathering up its supplies. In the days of Byron and Shelley, some seventy years ago, Wordsworth was held in contempt, and it seemed as if impiety ruled the realm of poetry. Yet how much since then of deep religious utterance, of pure and reverential meditation and aspiration, has been poured forth in high, rich strains of verse! Tennyson's day is not quite gone, and his has not been the music of despair. Browning's perplexities and paradoxes have opened forth into fruit of faith and worship. Myers is a true and high poet, whose work outshines in beauty the lurid splendors of the poetry of despair. Lewis Morris may not be a great poet, but he is in the true poetic succession, and may well be joined with Myers as showing the continuity of the tradition of faith among our contemporary poets. Yet a little while and greater names will prolong through after years the still growing galaxy of the poets of faith and holy awe, of reverence and hope and love. It cannot be that the great music of English poetry shall end only in despair. The heavenly sweetness of the song of Ariel seems lost ; but we mourn not as those without hope, for even while we cry with Ferdinand, " 'Tis gone," behold the air thrills again with magical vibration, and there is heard the faint prophetic cadence of a new song, divine and glorious as the olden, heralding the coming ages, and we cry also with Ferdinand, " No ; it begins again ! "

THE END.

www.ingramcontent.com/pod-product-compliance
Lightning Source LLC
Chambersburg PA
CBHW030102030726
47498CB00007B/2223